Contents

Thanks be to my critique group, my beta readers, the CTF, my saintly husband, my religious friends who can laugh at zealotry, my atheist friends who don't equate faith with ignorance, my confused agnostic friends, and, of course, the Almighty Comedian.

Disclaimer

This is a work of fiction and is not intended to be read as scripture. I, the author, make no claim of having a direct line to God. If I did have that, I would shamelessly exploit it for power and money, not for writing comedy.

THE BEGINNING

Jessica Christ, Book 1

H. CLAIRE TAYLOR

FFS
≡MEDIA≡

Chapter One

0 AGC

In the beginning, Jimmy had been so sure. There'd been no doubt in his mind that what he'd dreamed was more than just a dream; it was a conversation with Jesus himself. All Jimmy had to do was write it down as soon as he awoke, make a few tweaks here and there for dramatic effect, and so it was as the Good Lord intended. His prophecy. The Gospel according to Jimmy Dean. Or rather, the Gospel according to John Sonville, which was the alias he'd smartly adopted after the Utah fiasco. It was a shame that once the prophecy came to pass, no one but hordes of sinners would be around to remember that it was Jimmy who had been chosen by Jesus himself.

But at eleven fifty-five on July sixth, Jimmy wondered if maybe he'd misread the signs.

He'd find out in five minutes.

He gazed out over the temple of his own making—well,

someone else had built the barn, but he'd done most of the redecoration including the placement of plywood across the hay barrels to create pews that faced his chair at front and center. As he surveyed his beautiful, youthful flock, doubt jabbed at him again. What if this did just turn out to be Utah all over again? Was it possible that his dream about Jesus hadn't been more than that: a dream?

Just nerves, that's all. And who wouldn't be nervous, staring down the barrel of the apocalypse? Courage, don't fail me now!

The electric fans he'd placed around the barn, most of which he'd aimed at his designated seat, did little to combat the sweltering summer heat that persisted in the dead of night. If God was truly merciful, He'd have a few dozen pitchers of icy sweet tea waiting for when Jimmy and his flock arrived in Heaven. Maybe some whiskey, too.

He took a deep breath, closing his eyes and blocking out the sight of his creation to allow his mind to focus on something other than refreshing beverages and the doe-eyed girls waiting for … well, waiting for anything, any small morsel of wisdom or divinity he might provide. He could've scratched his balls and they would have tried to understand what it meant about Heaven and Hell. Not for the first time, he thanked God for granting him such a classically handsome nose, trustworthy eyes, silky-soft facial hair, and a naturally slim frame. He would have credited the latter to hard physical labor, except he'd ditched that dead-end way of life and hopped a train west from Mobile first chance he got, which, turned out, was a lot sooner than he'd expected. Nothing like puberty on the open road to help turn a boy into a man, he always said.

The girls fidgeted anxiously around him, but they didn't speak to one another. Managing to get a group of teenaged girls to sit quietly and not gossip was perhaps the greatest miracle of this entire heavenly undertaking, rivaling even Jesus's initial appearance in Jimmy's dream.

But if something went wrong, if the world wasn't ending, if he'd misinterpreted the dream, he'd need an even grander miracle to bail him out.

When he was younger and things had gone south, people around him would say, "It's not the end of the world. You'll be fine." But as a man of faith, Jimmy knew that the end of the world was *not* the worst-case scenario. In his present situation, the *continuation* of the world, not the end of it, could lead to the worst closing act of his long journey. Non-believers didn't take kindly to grown men gathering young, beautiful women around them and promising the blissful things Jimmy promised. Never mind that he'd never crossed the line with a single member of his flock. No one would buy that because no one ever understood the resolve of Jimmy Dean. He was nothing if not a man of moral fortitude.

The best-case scenario for him now was the apocalypse. Anything short could lead to an interstate manhunt and a shared jail cell.

He'd be long gone before anyone could catch his scent, though. Pure intentions and an honest mistake wouldn't be the cross he'd die on. He'd make sure of that.

The clock at the back of the barn ticked off the seconds until the end of the world or …

"Pastor Sonville."

Jimmy opened his eyes to find Emily standing just a few feet in front of his large wooden chair in the center of the makeshift chapel of plywood-and-hay pews. Peeking out from just behind Emily was her sister, younger by three years, a freshman in high school and perhaps still a few months away from the clutches of puberty.

He smiled gently at sweet, sweet Emily. She'd tested his restraint the most of all God's Virgins and had proven herself to be quite the maven. He credited the size of his following mostly to Emily's naturally persuasive abilities. She would be the first wife he would take in the afterlife. And with her staring so trustingly at him like that, the afterlife couldn't come soon enough. "Yes, daughter?"

"Samantha wants to know if the End will hurt. I told her it wouldn't, but she doesn't listen. Would you tell her like you told me?"

Jimmy nodded slowly and took a deep breath, filling his chest with the stale barn air and trying to savor it, since it would (hopefully) be one of the last breaths he took on this earth. As he stood confidently from his chair, Emily and Samantha stepped back—Emily in deference, Samantha perhaps in fear. So Jimmy smiled down at her to show there was nothing *to* fear. Well, besides the apocalypse.

But that was still four minutes away.

Once her hesitancy appeared to subside, he bent down till he was eye-level with the worried little girl and took both of her hands into one of his, and with his other hand lifted her chin with a crooked finger so that she met his gaze. "The End will be a purification more pleasant than anything you can imagine." He let those words sink in for a moment and congratulated himself, not for the first time, on this little detail he'd concocted toward the beginning of this particular religious undertaking. "It'll feel like a fire building inside you, starting just below your belly, building, building, getting warmer, more intense. That's God's mercy burning you up. Then you'll start to feel like you can't contain all of the mercy that He's thrusting into you for your loyalty to Him, and your body will feel like it's going to explode as pulses of His energy surge up your spine, making your toes curl, your back arch"—he glanced over at Emily to find that her face was even rosier than usual and her nostrils flared as she fidgeted and shifted on her heels—"the intensity with which His love is thrust into your heart might make you scream, but only because it feels so good and pure. And then suddenly it's all over. Poof!" He dotted her nose with his finger. "You're in Heaven with only the people in this barn by your side."

Samantha nodded minutely, her eyebrows raised high, her mouth dangling slightly open as she processed the information. "So it hurts?"

Jimmy rolled his eyes. With the clock this close to midnight and the anxiety inside him gathering like a storm, he lacked the patience needed to keep reassuring everyone. He stood up and returned to his chair. "Yes, but it's a good kind of hurt." He sat and draped his arms over the armrests, wrapping his fingers around the soft, carved wood.

"What about my friends who aren't in this barn?"

Samantha asked. "What if I want them to be in Heaven, too?"

He shrugged his shoulders curtly. "They missed the boat. They're going to burn in Hell for all eternity." He ignored Samantha's horrified gasp and let his eyes wander over the shiny hair of his blossoming followers until his attention was drawn to the clock on the wall. Only then did he realize that it might have been a smart, albeit subconscious, decision to place the clock *behind* the pews so that only he could see it from his position, while the girls all faced away. Eleven fifty-six. Not long now. His stomach burned.

God, fill me up with Your grace. I could use a little reassurance that this thing's actually going to happen.

There was no reply, nothing that could be interpreted as a sign. He really didn't want to move across the country again. After Utah, he'd promised himself he would settle down somewhere. Elbow, Texas, had seemed as good a place as any—remote, friendly, God-fearing. He never should have let himself get sucked into the business of religious leadership again. Somehow, leading a flock was both his greatest strength as well as his greatest weakness. It was all about the story, really. He was superb at creating a story, or at least the beginning and middle of a story. The end was always more difficult. And Jesus hadn't mentioned anything about an ending in the dream, either. So Jimmy had been forced to surmise, and the apocalypse seemed as good a finale as any.

Maybe recalling the dream again would help calm him

...

He was in bed in Utah, two particularly desirable ewes of his previous flock on either side of him, fulfilling wishes he'd long held but never acted upon. And then Jesus crashed the scene. There was the part where Jesus introduced himself, assured Jimmy that, yes, he was an Arab, and then it all got a little fuzzy from there, but Jimmy was sure that July seventh had been of some importance in the message. Something about a new dawn for Earth. Well, if Jesus was going to be cryptic, what choice did Jimmy have but to fill in the details?

So that's what he'd done.

New dawn for the world was clearly the apocalypse, right? That seemed obvious enough. Or at least it'd seemed obvious enough in the ten months between when Jimmy had woken up in a cold sweat and when he'd amassed this flock of young, pretty things into the barn for the final countdown (fingers crossed!).

Jesus? You there? Grant me a sign that the end is near. Anything helps.

He waited for a surge of confidence. It didn't come. That was unfortunate. But he knew what would cheer him up. "God's Virgins. Gather round."

The young women, mostly upperclassmen from Elbow High School, knew that was their cue. Earlier that morning, as he enjoyed what he hoped would be his last sausage-and-egg breakfast ever, he'd counted in his head twenty girls who would show up in the barn later that night. But now that he looked around, there seemed to be only eighteen. Who was missing? He wracked his memory, running through the list chronologically from who he'd recruited first to who in his flock had joined most recently. Ah, Kimber and Misty, that's who was missing. Their parents always *were* a little too suspicious of his youth group. And now those poor girls would be the ones to pay for it by missing the one-way boxcar to Heaven. Maybe. Assuming he'd been correct in his interpretation. No matter. Eighteen was still plenty of God's Virgins for him to enjoy in the afterlife. As time ticked down toward midnight, Jimmy's anxiety grew.

"Come closer and pray with me." The teens gathered round, got as close to Jimmy as they could so that each could rest a hand on him to soak up his Divine Promise. He closed his eyes and felt a chill run down his spine when one of his ewes rested a palm on his inner thigh.

Thank you, God, for blessing me with this responsibility. Please don't screw me over.

"Pray with me, ladies."

At eleven fifty-eight on July sixth, they bowed their heads.

"Lord Almighty, the one who grants our prayers, who speaks to me through our savior Jesus Christ, this is Your prophet coming to You with my flock. They thank You for giving them such a kind, generous, tender leader. This humble servant of Yours will not falter in his responsibility of guiding Your virgins up to Heaven and showing them Your rock-solid mercy in the hereafter. Please, Lord Father, take these young ladies up into Your arms and reward them for being such good servants of Your word. And of my word. Amen."

The girls echoed the amen.

"Keep your heads bowed, now." He looked at the clock. Eleven fifty-nine. The flow of uncertainty was increasing more by the minute, and he wondered if the dam would give way. Prayer hadn't soothed him. The seconds ticked down. "God's Virgins, you must all hold hands in a circle in the center of the room. Then, uh, close your eyes. Most importantly, resist the temptation to put your hands on my body." The girls removed their hands from him and created a circle, as instructed, though it was clear to Jimmy that they were unsure where in the teachings this practice originated.

"Eyes shut," he said again. "Keep them shut tight. When the end comes, God will shine down a light so bright that it will feel like Hellfire in your eye sockets if your eyes aren't *completely* closed."

That did the trick. And once no one could see him, he stood from his chair as quietly as he could.

"Only a few more seconds, everyone." He tiptoed toward the barn doors. "Pray as hard as you can. So hard. Spread yourself wide for God's mercy."

When he glanced up at the clock on the wall and saw the hands align at midnight, he held his breath for the length of a couple seconds.

But nothing happened.

He was disappointed, yes. But he was also relieved. For a moment he wondered if that meant he doubted the prophecy himself, or worse, doubted his belief in the afterlife. Or even *worse,* believed in the afterlife but doubted he'd make the cut for the Eternal Fun Place with lots of whiskey and sweet tea and pretty women and no talk of either marriage or taxes.

He was also immediately glad of a few things. First, he was glad he hadn't splurged on the large grandfather clock he'd had his eye on the week before, the one that chimed ominously on the hour. Second, he was glad he hadn't prematurely indulged in any of his Heaven fantasies, since it was clear the girls weren't passing into the next life anytime soon and he hadn't bothered to look up the age of consent in these parts. But mostly he was glad he hadn't sold his truck.

As his flock remained silent, eyes closed, heads bowed, apparently unaware that midnight had come and gone uneventfully, a thought struck him that gave him pause. Maybe the clock on the wall was fast. He pulled his cell phone from his pocket and checked on there. Shit. The clock on the wall was off, but only because it was two minutes *behind*. So he was just flat out wrong about the apocalypse. Well, live and learn, he supposed. But what about the dream?

It was just a dream, you dumb ass. Just like in Utah.

That was unfortunate, really. One of his few talents was organizing people, gathering them to him. Unless he was going to get into politics, which just seemed intolerably sleazy to him, the best use of his gift was to start a church.

He'd been wrong before, sure, but the dream with Jesus and the ewes had seemed different somehow—more real.

It didn't matter now. It was obvious that unless God functioned on Mountain or Pacific time, the apocalypse wasn't coming tonight, which meant he needed to skedaddle before these girls went and spilled everything to their parents.

He opened the barn door only a foot, just enough for his slender body to slip through and escape into the night air. He had to get gone, and soon. The question was, where to?

He couldn't go back to his rundown apartment—not that he really wanted to. Parents would be looking for him before long. He needed to get out of Elbow, probably even out of Texas.

His instincts told him to head east—way east—not just away from Elbow, but farther away from Hatch, Utah, too. But he couldn't stand easterners with their lack of hospitality and hearty dose of skepticism. Just plain unpleasant to be around, and ungodly to boot.

Maybe he could head north, up into Oklahoma and then on into Nebraska.

And do what? Freeze to death?

He sighed resignedly when he thought of Hank. Hank owed him big time from their young and reckless days. It was unfortunate that Hank was in Carlsbad, though, because that meant heading back toward Utah.

Jimmy made it to his pickup truck, climbed in quickly but quietly, and started the engine. As he threw the truck into drive and began pulling away down the dirt road, he glanced in his rearview mirror. The first few of the girls wandered out of the barn and were bathed in the red of his taillights. They ambled around like sleepwalkers as they watched him leave.

Eh, they'd figure it out soon enough. They were fairly smart girls, and resilient. Probably.

Once his former flock was no longer visible in the rearview mirror, his mind drifted back to Jesus. Now that he knew it was *just* a dream, parts of it started to make more sense. *Of course* Jesus wouldn't appear to him in a dream. That seemed like a backdoor way into someone's mind, and if Jesus was who the Bible made him out to be, he could just show up at Jimmy's doorstep and start barking orders. But he hadn't.

And then there were the instructions that Jesus had given him. "If you build it, she will come." It *did* seem strange that Jesus's message would rip off *Field of Dreams* only a few hours after Jimmy had watched it for the first time. That sounded more like a trick of his simple, mortal brain. And now that he was really deconstructing it, the odds seemed high that he'd simply interpreted that phrase to mean exactly what he wanted it to mean.

The dark country roads leading out of Elbow, Texas, were in desperate need of maintenance. His Tacoma bobbed up and down as it rolled over one pothole after another in a rhythm that was almost but not quite relaxing, like when he was a boy being bounced on his pastor's knee as the man taught of the Holy Spirit. Jimmy could still see, quite vividly, the face of Pastor Heathrow staring down at him. A related memory knocked from behind a padlocked door in his mind, but Jimmy decided to ignore it like he always did, and a moment later the truck hit a real doozy of a pothole and the jolt rattled his skull and made him curse.

No way that hadn't done at least a little damage to his front axle.

After a half-hour of the rough roads, he made it to the nice, paved highway and headed west toward New Mexico. The smooth ride allowed him to finally take a deep breath as the events of the past ten months started to sink in. There was no denying it had been an entertaining time.

Nothing good is made to last.

He sighed and turned his mind to his future. No point in dwelling on the past. The past had become irrelevant at midnight. But there was usually a silver lining he could find, another opportunity awaiting him. Maybe he could be happy in Carlsbad. It hadn't been the worst time when he'd stayed there with Hank before. Plus, the people there would believe anything, really. If they'd buy into aliens, he could win them over to God. It'd worked on Hank. Jimmy would just have to scale up.

He'd have to think of a new name. People would be looking for John Sonville. They might still be looking for Oscar, the name he'd used in Utah. Maybe it was time to go all in and use his real name. Perhaps the aliases were a way of keeping one foot on land when what he needed to do, if he were ever to succeed in his calling, was to put both feet in the God-blessed boat and let the winds carry him onward to meet his destiny—not as John or Oscar, but as Jimmy.

He looked at his reflection in the rearview mirror. Once he shaved off the thick facial hair, he'd be almost unrecognizable. That was good. He never looked as wise when he was clean shaven, but he was much more handsome, which was equally as effective for recruitment, even if it required a different approach.

His eyes moved back to the lonely stretch of road just in time to see something large sitting right in the middle of the double yellow lines. Jimmy's reflexes made an executive decision that the object was far too large to simply run over, so he swerved to avoid hitting it, veering off the pavement and into a ditch that hardly counted as a shoulder. His airbag deployed as his truck nosedived into the trench and stopped abruptly.

The impact left his ears ringing, but outside of that, he was surrounded by silence. What the hell *was* that on the road?

He swatted the rapidly deflating airbag out of his way, did a quick mental sweep of his body to make sure there were no serious injuries, then grabbed his shotgun from behind the seat and crawled out of the truck.

Kicked-up dirt swirled in his headlights as he peered out at the dark road trying to spot the animal that had caused this crash. Assuming it wasn't a human being, it'd be a good gift to bring Hank out in Carlsbad when he showed up looking for a place to stay. Maybe it was a deer. That could make for some good sausage. But no, he'd hit deer with his truck before without much more than a little blood, a minor dent in his hood, and a few scratches to the paint. He doubted his reflexes would have told him to swerve if it were just a deer.

As he squinted through the darkness, a voice boomed to his right.

"JIMMY."

He whirled around toward the scrub brush on the side of the road, gun aimed ahead, only to find a huge hog staring back at him. Ah, that made more sense. Damn, that was a huge hog. Had he ever seen one so large, even in this part of the country? He was glad he'd swerved, even if it did leave him in a bit of a pickle with his truck. Hitting a feral pig that size could've spelled the end for both parties.

He knew he should just unload into the beast right away—these things were real assholes if you gave them a chance—but he could've sworn he'd just heard the hog say his name.

No. That was crazy. He brought the shotgun up to eye level, lining up the sights on the hog's skull.

But the beast didn't charge. Instead, its mouth moved as it spoke. "JIMMY DEAN."

"What ... the fuck?" Before Jimmy could say anything else, the hog turned and trotted off into the brush.

He couldn't just shoot a hog who'd spoken his name— his real one, no less—his curiosity wouldn't let him.

He hesitated as a schism developed in his mind. On the one hand, this was a strange occurrence that should be looked into further. On the other hand, this was probably what a psychotic break felt like.

But he pursued into the brush anyway.

The farther from the lights of his truck he went, the more his eyes were able to adjust to the darkness, allowing him to better track the movement of the hog. He came upon a small rocky clearing in the landscape and in the middle of it stood the feral animal, staring right at him. He considered the merits of just shooting the damn thing, drinking away the memory, and being done with it, but no. He'd see this thing out a bit more before doing anything too rash.

"JIMMY," the hog spoke again in a voice that was booming and rich without being loud. Its mouth moved like a pig's would, but somehow it was able to create a human voice. "I AM GOD."

Jimmy wasn't expecting that, although he probably should've been. "The hell you say?"

"DID I STUTTER?"

Well shit, thought Jimmy. "Uh, no. I just ... what do You want?"

"IS THAT HOW YOU TALK TO THE LORD?"

"I guess so. Sorry. I just didn't expect this."

"SAYS THE MAN WHO ONCE STARTED A CHURCH BECAUSE HE THOUGHT I SPOKE TO HIM THROUGH CLOUDS."

Jimmy frowned and scratched his head. "Ah okay. Well, just so I'm clear on this, bunnies *aren't* reincarnated centurions?"

"NOPE."

"Well, damn."

The hog snorted and flapped its tail. "JIMMY, I HAVE AN IMPORTANT MISSION FOR YOU."

Jimmy held his breath as the reality finally crashed down on him like a tidal wave: he was in the presence of the Lord. *The* Lord. The one who made him. And women. And the hog through which He now spoke.

The moniker of "Almighty Hogmaker" clanked around

Jimmy's skull like a piece of toxic plaque shaking free from his brain.

He snapped to attention, hoping not to screw things up too terribly.

"TONIGHT MY SECOND CHILD IS BORN. I NEED YOU TO FIND THE MOTHER AND LET HER KNOW THAT SHE IS GIVING BIRTH TO THE CHILD OF GOD."

"Whatever you say, God. But why me?"

"BECAUSE YOU ARE THE ONLY ONE WITHIN FIFTY MILES OF THE NATIVITY WHO'S NARCISSISTIC ENOUGH TO BELIEVE THAT GOD IS TALKING TO YOU THROUGH A HOG."

Hm. That was *almost* a compliment from God Himself, so Jimmy would take it.

"WILL YOU DO THIS?"

"Do I have a choice?" The question was much more profound than he'd intended.

"YOU ALWAYS HAVE A CHOICE. BUT YOUR OPTIONS ARE EITHER RELAY THE MESSAGE OR BE SMITED."

"Okay, then. I choose the first option." He swallowed hard, sweat beading around his hairline. "Tell me what to do."

The hog said nothing more as it walked toward Jimmy, passed him, then headed back toward the truck. Not wanting to accidentally agitate God, Jimmy refrained from asking any more questions as he turned and followed.

When he arrived back at his vehicle, he almost couldn't believe what he saw. His Tecoma was no longer in the ditch but was instead idling softly on the road, its hazards flashing steadily. Jimmy's shock quickly transitioned into paranoia, and he leveled his shotgun on his hip and squinted into the dark in every direction, searching for whoever had moved his ride.

"IT'S A MIRACLE, STUPID."

He turned to look at the hog. "Huh?"

"A MIRACLE. YOUR TRUCK IS HEALED. NOW OPEN THE DOOR AND GIVE ME A LIFT UP, WILL YOU?"

Jimmy ran to open the passenger's side door as God waited patiently next to it. He looked back and forth from the hog to the seat before pursing his lips, scooting the scoop seat back as far as it would go, and hoping that was enough room between it and the dashboard.

He moved to the side to allow God room to climb in, but quickly realized the limitations of the swine body and wondered if he was supposed to help.

He took a quick step forward. "Do You need, um, should I ... ?"

"UH YEAH."

"So wait. You can move a truck out of a ditch, but You can't get Yourself into the seat of said truck?"

"YES."

Jimmy scratched his hairline with the barrel of the shotgun. "Now that just doesn't make sense."

"I WORK IN MYSTERIOUS WAYS. AND THIS IS THE FIRST HOG I'VE EVER WORN. NOW ARE YOU DONE QUESTIONING THE LORD, OR SHOULD I STRETCH MY SMITING MUSCLE?"

Jimmy held up his hand defensively as he leaned the shotgun against the tire. "No need. Forgive me, O Lord."

Then he inhaled deeply and squatted down to grab the beast, unsure how successful he would actually be in lifting what was easily a three-hundred pound animal.

He tried to wrap his arms around the hog's middle, but the thing was just too damn round. Maybe if he could just scoop it up …

When he slid his arms underneath God's belly, he cringed as his hand brushed against the hog's penis.

"WATCH IT."

Jimmy straightened up to reassess his strategy. "I'm trying! I've never lifted a hog *or* a god before."

"THERE IS NO GOD BUT ME."

Responding to that seemed like a bad idea, so instead, Jimmy focused on the task at hand. He used the shoulder of his cotton shirt to wipe the sweat from his brow and then squatted again and managed to lift the front half of the animal so that the hooves were on the seat. Next, he reached down to the back half, this time more mindful of the genitals. With a grunt, Jimmy hoisted the hog's rear, his thighs straining with the heavy load.

But finally, God was in the passenger's seat. Jimmy took a deep breath and tried not to think too hard about any of this as he slammed the door and walked around to the driver's side. He hopped in, tossed the shotgun into the backseat, but couldn't quite bring himself to look to his right as he asked, "Okay, where to?"

"MOORETOWN."

Jimmy had heard of it before but never been there, mostly because there was never a reason to go. From what he knew of the place, people did their best to *leave*

Mooretown rather than travel to it. He looked over at the hog and felt a sudden obligation to buckle it up, so he leaned over, reached across, and grabbed the seatbelt. Being in such close proximity to an animal that he usually tried his best to avoid left him incredibly uneasy. He wasn't sure if the fact that it was inhabited by God made him more or less anxious, or really what he *should* be feeling. On the one hand, he was in the presence of God, but on the other, God had a weird pig penis that Jimmy had accidentally touched …

"WHAT ARE YOU DOING?" God asked as Jimmy clumsily pulled the seatbelt around Him.

"I'm trying to be responsible!"

"MAYBE YOU DON'T UNDERSTAND THAT I'M *GOD*. I WON'T DIE IN A CAR ACCIDENT."

Shit, shit, shit! Jimmy's nerves were fraying big-time—it'd already been a long night, and all he wanted to do was be safe and sound in Carlsbad with a beer in one hand and maybe some good vintage porn in the other, the kind where the women weren't fully naked so it wasn't such a sin.

But instead, he buckled himself up and put the Tacoma into drive. God Hog gave booming directions and Jimmy followed them, wondering if the world actually *had* ended at midnight and this was the afterlife.

Mooretown was about an hour's drive away, and Jimmy knew that this might be the only chance he ever got to speak with God one-on-one. No pressure, though. Unfortunately, all the burning questions he'd formulated over the course of his life were obliterated by more pressing ones he'd never anticipated asking, like *Why me?*

and *How are you moving the hog's lips like that?* and *Why a hog?* and *Couldn't you make the hog smell a little better?* But all those questions seemed imprudent, even with his judgment as befuddled as it was.

So instead, he asked the question that seemed least rude. "Will I ever make it to Carlsbad?"

"OH, I'M SORRY, DID YOU THINK I WAS SOME CHEAP FORTUNE TELLER?"

"No, I just—"

"YOU WILL NEVER MAKE IT TO CARLSBAD. YOU WILL NEVER LEAVE TEXAS AGAIN."

"Shit."

"SHIT INDEED."

Something about a curse word coming from the Lord's mouth sent icy shivers down Jimmy's spine. He almost didn't have the courage to keep speaking. Almost. "So that dream. That wasn't a message from you?"

The hog snorted and it almost sounded like a laugh. "NO. THAT WAS NOT ME." Then after a short pause. "THAT WAS JESUS."

"Jesus? But wait, I thought You, like, *were* Jesus and vice versa."

"THAT DOESN'T EVEN MAKE SENSE. JESUS IS MY CHILD. HOW COULD I BE HIM? THAT'S CREEPY."

Jimmy shrugged. "Yeah, I always thought so, too." He glanced over at God, momentarily forgetting that a hog would be there, felt a small jolt of panic when he saw it, and then quickly returned his eyes to the road.

"JESUS LIKES TO VISIT PEOPLE IN THEIR DREAMS. HE'S ALL INTO THAT. I DON'T

UNDERSTAND IT. BUT CHILDREN ARE THEIR OWN PEOPLE, YOU KNOW?"

"Uh, not really. I don't have any—" but then he remembered who he was talking to. Was that a pang of guilt he felt in his gut or the early stages of a good smiting?

He needed to change the subject. "So, what do I say when I get there?"

"YOU'LL KNOW. DON'T WORRY ABOUT IT."

"Don't worry about— I'm supposed to tell a *woman giving birth* that God is her baby daddy, and You don't want me to worry about how that'll go over?"

"I EXPECT SHE'LL BE RELIEVED TO KNOW WHO THE FATHER IS."

This was not the merciful God that Jimmy had always believed in. This was not even the wrathful God that Jimmy had worried might exist. This was just unhelpful God. Maybe even lackadaisical God.

"What if she doesn't listen?"

"ENOUGH QUESTIONS. DO YOU KNOW HOW HARD IT IS TO MAKE A HOG'S VOCAL CORDS MOVE LIKE THIS?"

Jimmy did not. "One more question."

The hog farted. "JUST ONE MORE."

"Could You make a rock that even You can't lift?"

"OOO I COULD JUST SMITE YOU. WE'RE DONE HERE. LEFT AT THE LIGHT."

Jimmy was pretty sure God wouldn't smite him before he'd completed his mission, but he decided to shut up anyway. God *wanting* to smite him was dangerous enough.

Mooretown had just one stoplight, and at this hour, that

stoplight was flashing red in all directions as Jimmy took the left God commanded and pulled into a small subdivision of double-wides.

Burglar lights flicked on from the front of each dark house as the truck drove by one lot after another.

"THERE." God grunted and lifted a hoof, pointing at the only house on the row with a soft glow emanating through the window blinds.

As they pulled into the driveway, Jimmy could already hear the coarse screams and low moans wafting from inside the mobile home. Having never stuck around long enough to see the birth of any of his children, he wasn't sure what to expect once he was actually inside, witnessing the miracle.

"HURRY."

Jimmy sighed, undid his seatbelt, and jumped out of the truck, marching purposefully to the front door, trying not to overthink what he might say. Because there was no point. He had to do this, no matter how badly he might botch it and make a fool of himself.

He knocked decisively on the front door and, while waiting for a response, noticed a carved wooden sign in the shape of a rainbow and puffy clouds hanging next to the door. *McCloud Family* was painted along the rainbow, the colors faded by time.

The door swung open, and a squat woman who looked to be either a haggard thirty-something or a baby-faced fifty-something eyed him up and down. "You better not be a salesman."

He could hear the yelling continuing somewhere behind

her, much louder now that the door was open, but he still couldn't see the actual source of the hollering. "Uh, no, I'm not a salesman."

"You the daddy?" She eyed him disapprovingly. "I'd hoped for someone richer."

"No, I'm not the daddy."

"Then what the fucking shit do you want?! Can't you hear my daughter's having a baby inside?"

Jimmy shifted restlessly from one foot to the other. "That's why I'm here, actually. I have a message from God about that baby."

The woman rolled her eyes so hard her head rocked back as well, and she blew a raspberry before slamming the door in his face.

Jimmy stood stunned for a moment before turning to look back at the truck. God was still in the front seat, staring at him. The hog blew on the windshield to fog it, then with its hoof wrote "SMITE" backward, so that Jimmy could read it forward. Okay. He got the message.

He knocked again.

More forceful, this time, Jimmy!

The string of profanities continued flowing from inside the home, sucking Jimmy in like a seductive incantation. He jumped when the door finally opened again inches from his face.

The gruff woman stood with a shotgun leveled at Jimmy's chest, and the air bolted out of his lungs in a whoosh.

"We don't call 9-1-1 here, mister, so you best have a good reason to knock again once I sent you along."

"I've come here—" His throat went dry. He swallowed and tried again, this time louder, more assertive. "I'm here on a mission from God. He sent me to deliver news about the girl's baby."

"*God* sent you, did He?" The woman cackled. "Well, send Him my best when you see Him face-to-face in about five seconds."

Because God really was about a five-second walk away from the doorstep—something only Jimmy knew, of course —the implication of her words didn't hit him right away.

But then, "Oh, you're going to shoot me."

"Mama!" came the voice from the living room. "Let him in! *Fuckin' shit shit shit shit!*"

The gruff woman shouted into the house, "You got enough to be dealing with without some jackhole coming in here telling you that God got you pregnant!"

The immediate reply from the girl was another string of profanities ending in, "Let him in! I wanna hear what he has to say."

The woman at the door lowered the shotgun slightly but continued to eye him suspiciously. "Fine, get your ass in, but don't try anything funny." She moved to the side so Jimmy could scoot by her.

He should have felt relieved that he'd passed the gatekeeper, but all he felt was dread, like he was walking up onto something he could never unsee.

That was truer than he'd guessed.

The source of all the commotion was on her hands and knees on a small pallet of towels in the middle of the living room floor. Strings of straight ash-brown hair formed a tattered, sweaty veil over her face. Her head stuck out from underneath a white sheet draped over her back, extending from just below the shoulders, down her legs, to right above the ankles, covering all her shameful bits from Jimmy's view.

This was *not* how he'd ever imagined childbirth. Not human childbirth, at least. "Jesus," he whispered.

The girl sucked in air in jagged bursts. "You got something to say?" she asked, hardly interrupting her rhythm of Lamaze and cursing.

"Yeah. I–I—" He closed his eyes and tried to steady himself against the nausea brewing in his gut. "I'm here to tell you that the child you give birth to tonight will be the child of God Himself."

"See, Destinee?" said the gruff woman. "This is why I told him to scram."

Destinee grunted and pushed, then started breathing heavily again. "No, Ma, it's good. It's good. Now at least we know who the"—she yelled, a guttural sound that reminded Jimmy of some primal cry from eons ago—"the father is. I'm just glad it's not Jason or Kyle"—she hollered again—"or Caydon or"—more yelling—"Garrett or Denton."

She flipped her soaking hair back over her shoulder, and a pained but excited expression overtook her round face. Her squinty eyes grew squintier. "Oh shit, Mama! I think it's happening!"

The soon-to-be-grandma dropped her shotgun and ran to her daughter, kneeling behind her before diving under the blanket to guide the baby the rest of the way out.

Jimmy's knees buckled and he collapsed onto a plastic-covered armchair and watched the sheet undulate before him as various body parts of mother and daughter poked out in different directions.

Forgive me, God, for ever putting a woman through this. The prayer was a habit, nothing more. But Jimmy made a mental note to say it to God's face once he got back in his truck.

The screaming and grunting seemed like it'd never end, until finally it was pierced by a cry of a different pitch.

It was the first sounds of life from the second coming.

Tears welled in Jimmy's eyes, and he felt lightheaded. The now-grandmother made quick work of cutting and tying off the umbilical cord before she wrapped a clean sheet around Destinee and helped guide her down onto her back, head resting on a stack of couch cushions, slime-covered baby crying on her chest.

The gravity of the situation was starting to settle in. Jimmy had just witnessed the birth of the Christ Child. His eyes roamed the baby's body, trying to rectify the awe he knew he *should* feel with what he was actually seeing. "Is he supposed to be covered in all that muck?"

But no one responded. Destinee stared down at her child in a blissful haze, and her mother was too busy wiping off the goo and disposing of the cord to pay Jimmy any mind.

And then, once most of the slime had been wiped clean, Destinee's mother carried the umbilical cord and soiled sheets out of the living room, leaving Destinee to clutch the child close to her breast and croon soft words Jimmy couldn't make out from where he sat in the plastic-covered chair.

In that peaceful moment Jimmy realized something: Destinee was *young*. Perhaps she was on the older side of God's Virgins, but she definitely *looked* like she was toward the younger end.

So God preferred them fresh too, huh? Jimmy supposed he should have known that, considering how young Mary had been. But things had been different back then, and for some reason, he'd assumed God would have changed with the times.

I guess some things are eternal.

He was tugged from his thoughts by Destinee's calm but hoarse voice. "What's your name?"

"Jimmy."

"I'm Destinee. You can come closer if you want."

Jimmy approached slowly and knelt down next to where Destinee rested against the stack of couch cushions. "Is it supposed to look like that?" he asked.

Destinee's squinty eyes popped open in alarm, and her attention snapped to his face immediately. "Like what?"

"Like a little old man."

The girl laughed. "Oh. I got no fucking clue."

"Should you be cursing … ?" He motioned with his eyes at the baby.

"Oh. Maybe not." She kept her gaze on the newborn as she asked, "You really think she's the daughter of God?"

"He. Son," Jimmy corrected.

Destinee looked at him skeptically, then gently lifted the baby off her chest so that he could get a good look.

Wait. Where's the pecker?

He was no expert, but he was fairly sure a pecker was something male babies were born with, not something that grew in later. "I ... don't understand." Could there have been a mix-up? Could he have come to the wrong house that just happened to have a woman giving birth? Could God be bad with directions?

"That's a cooch," Destinee said plainly. "So it's a girl."

"But then ..." He looked down at the baby. Yep. Cooter for sure. He scratched his head.

Did I make the whole thing up?

"Hold on." He stood, walked to the front door, opened it a crack, and peeked out at the truck. The hog was still sitting there. It puffed onto the windshield and the word *SMITE* appeared again.

"Dammit!" Jimmy waved off the hog and went back inside.

When he walked into the living room, Destinee's mother was back, kneeling next to her and doting on the baby.

"I think I'll name her Jessica," said Destinee, rubbing the baby's back.

Grandma nodded approvingly. "Jessica McCloud. I like it."

"No," said the new mom, looking at Jimmy then back at her mother. "Jessica Christ."

Destinee's mother raised one eyebrow and looked over at Jimmy, who could do nothing but shrug apologetically.

"We'll talk about it," she said, making it clear this was not the final word on the matter.

"If you'll just excuse me," Jimmy said, backing toward the front door, "I think I've done what I came to do."

"You don't have to leave," said Destinee, staring up at him. "Mama could make you some coffee or something."

It was clear from Mrs. McCloud's face that she would do no such thing, but that was just as well, considering Jimmy had no plans to keep God waiting longer than he had to.

"Thanks, but I really should be leaving. My, uh, my work here is done." He forced an awkward smile.

Destinee nodded understandingly and waved good-bye while Mrs. McCloud just waved him away.

He exited the double-wide and shut the door behind him, and as he looked out at the truck, the hog still waiting in the front seat, it became quite clear to him that although he might be a messenger of the Lord, the only message he had to deliver to the world was one he very much doubted the world wanted to hear: God had a *daughter*. A *Texan* daughter.

He pulled up the front collar of his cotton shirt and dragged it over his face from forehead to chin.

Well, when people didn't want to hear your message, you just had to tweak the message, he supposed. He'd done it twice before and he could do it again. And this time he'd succeed.

He walked back to his truck to face God Himself and hopefully wrap up what had been a long, confusing, and nerve-wracking night.

But he paused before opening the driver's side door and gazed through the window into the cab. The tip of God's tail stuck out to the side of His fat ass and wagged quickly, flapping back and forth like it was struggling to free itself from the crushing weight pinning it down.

God was excited. That made Jimmy excited, too.

The night hadn't been about the End of Days at all; it had been about the beginning. It was the dawn of a new age, just like Jesus had said while Jimmy was sandwiched between those two Utahan hotties in that dream.

A grin snuck onto Jimmy's lips for the first time since he'd seen the clock strike midnight not even two hours before.

With every ending came a new beginning and with every new beginning came a world of opportunity.

Reverend Jimmy Dean, he thought, grabbing the door handle. He liked the sound of that.

Chapter Two

---

5 AGC

"I only remember bits and pieces of kindergarten," Destinee McCloud said as she walked her daughter the three and a half blocks to Mooreson Elementary. "But from what I remember, it wasn't all horrible. You'll make lots of new friends and your teacher is really nice. I already spoke with her and she's excited to meet you."

"Did you tell her about Dad?" Jess asked, keeping her eyes on the sidewalk to avoid stepping on the seams between cement squares.

Destinee stopped and turned Jess around to face her before kneeling to be at eye level. "No. I didn't tell her about that. And remember what I told you to say when people ask about your daddy?"

Jess gazed over Destinee's shoulder as she tried to recall the exact words she'd been coached on. "I tell them, 'My daddy is in Heaven.'"

"And you mean it when you say it, Jess."

"But I don't understand why I can't just tell them the truth."

"That *is* the truth, Jess. Your daddy is in Heaven. End of story. Trust me, baby, you're not going to like the way people react if you tell them you're"—she glanced around to make sure no one was nearby, then lowered her voice—"the daughter of God."

"God doesn't like me denying him."

Destinee pursed her lips and stood. "Absent daddies don't get a say in what their daughters do."

"He's not absent," Jess said.

"Well, he sure ain't paying child support, and until he starts doing that, I make the rules around here."

This wasn't the first time Jessica had heard this complaint, and she knew there was no point in responding once her mom started talking about it.

So she returned her focus to the day's big challenge. She didn't necessarily dread starting kindergarten, but she also didn't feel especially excited about it. It seemed unimportant. But maybe it would be fun. She was nervous about being away from her mom for so long every day—with Destinee technically working from home, albeit as a telemarketer, Jess hadn't ever had to endure days in childcare. Instead, she'd spent most of her hours watching nature shows on TV by herself or playing safari with her stuffed animals by herself or coloring pictures of her favorite animals that Destinee had printed from the Internet. Again, by herself. She was curious to find out what it would be like to play with other kids her age.

As Mooreson Elementary loomed closer, swarmed by hordes of students and parents, Jess grew anxious and receded into her mind for comfort. Unfortunately, though, in her mind, God was on another one of His soapboxes that little Jess knew so well.

... NOT REALLY NECESSARY FOR YOU TO START SCHOOL THIS YOUNG.

Half of what He said didn't make sense to her, because while she was quite mature for her age—necessity made it so—she had only just turned five.

"Maybe you'll meet your first crush, today, Jess!" said Destinee excitedly, squeezing Jessica's hand.

DON'T EVEN THINK ABOUT BOYS, CHILD.

But of course Jessica had no reference for what the heck her parents were talking about. Crush? What did that mean? Was she going to crush a boy? Was that something she could do?

Am I going to crush someone?

NO. YOU WON'T CRUSH ANYONE AND YOU WON'T HAVE A CRUSH ON ANYONE. THOU SHALT NOT CRUSH ON BOYS, HAVE I MADE MYSELF CLEAR?

Sure. Promising him she wouldn't crush anyone seemed easy enough.

"Is he talking to you again?" Destinee asked.

Jessica nodded.

"While you have him on the line, would you kindly remind him that his little miracle of knocking me up is great and all, but even Cheyenne Forte's good-for-nothing baby daddy chips in with the bills every once in a while, so ..." She let the words linger as she raised her eyebrows.

She wants money again.

YEAH, I HEARD HER. TELL HER, UH, THE LOVE OF MONEY IS THE ROOT OF ALL EVIL.

"He says that love of money is the root of all evil."

Destinee huffed exasperatedly and pulled Jessica behind her along the crosswalk. "Tell him— No, you know what? I can tell him. Because"—she looked around again to make sure no one would overhear—"*I know you can hear me. Stop avoiding me. You know you owe me something.*"

Jessica listened for God's voice, but He had gone silent again.

"He's ignoring you," she told her mom.

Her mother's grip on her hand tightened. "Omniscient but ignores the mother of his child. So much for the Heavenly Father bit."

Destinee had always referred to Mooretown as small, but to Jess, it'd constituted her entire world, and now that she approached the buildings and realized how many unfamiliar faces lived nearby, she wondered how small her town could really be. She'd never seen so many people in one place.

She tugged her mother's arm gently. "What if no one likes me?"

I WILL SMITE THEM. JUST GIVE ME THE WORD.

"You'll be fine, baby. You're sweet and you'll make plenty of friends."

SPEAKING OF FRIENDS, THERE'S SOMETHING I SHOULD TELL YOU ...

Jessica waited for it. God sure loved a dramatic reveal.

TODAY YOU'LL MAKE A LIFELONG FRIEND WHO WILL

REGULARLY BETRAY YOU, EVEN THOUGH SHE DOESN'T MEAN TO.

That doesn't sound like much of a friend. Can't you change that?

I, UH … SORRY, I FORGOT THERE'S AN EARTHQUAKE SCHEDULED IN THE HIMALAYAS RIGHT NOW. GOT TO GO.

She wasn't sure what the Himalayas were, but she recognized an excuse when she heard one. And it wasn't the first time God had used that exact one.

The hallways were packed shoulder to shoulder, and Jess stayed a step behind Destinee, following in her wake, clutching her hand until they turned and went inside a classroom.

"This is it," Destinee said, smiling down at Jessica.

Jess took in the surroundings. There were an awful lot of colors in there. It almost made her eyes hurt. She was used to the brown wood paneling on the walls at home, the faded blankets thrown over plastic-covered furniture, the framed pastel cross-stitches on the wall, the dim light creeping between the blinds in the morning and the glow of the streetlight radiating in around bedtime. All this color made her angry and alert.

"What is *that?*" she asked, pointing to a cartoon on the wall.

"I think that's supposed to be a giraffe. Or donkey? I'm not really sure."

"That's not what they look like on Animal Planet!" There was that anger seeping through.

"It's just a cartoon," Destinee said, trying to calm her down.

Jessica harrumphed at that and began inspecting her classmates. Then her eyes landed on a short, stocky woman with tight umber curls framing her puffy face. The woman was listening to a boy prattle on about something that he seemed to believe was crucially important, but her eyes were glued to Jessica.

Jess didn't like it. It was like the woman believed Jess would reveal the answer to some ancient riddle, if only the woman stared at her long enough.

Then the boy tugged on the woman's skirt, and her attention snapped back to him.

Destinee followed Jess's gaze. "That's Mrs. Thomas, your teacher. You'll like her. Her daughter's in this class, too. Here, let's go meet her."

Destinee dragged her over to greet her teacher, and Jess protested only slightly by lagging a step behind.

As soon as they stood a few feet from Mrs. Thomas, the teacher waved off the boy and turned her attention to them, first greeting Destinee before crouching down to get on eye level with Jess. She placed a warm hand on each of Jess's arms. "You must be Jessica!"

Jess nodded.

"I've heard so much about you! I'm so excited to have you in my class! It's going to be a great year."

Once she stood back up and began chatting with Destinee, Jess pulled on her mother's arm to ask permission to scram. Destinee understood, nodded, and let go of her hand.

A couple of kids were sitting at a tiny table toward the far corner of the classroom, coloring with crayons. That was something Jess knew she could do. She wondered what kinds of animals there were to color.

The small chair felt funny to sit in, but she did it anyway, only to realize that there were no coloring pages, only blank sheets. But there were plenty of crayons, and Jess had colored enough giraffes to know their shape by heart, so she grabbed a brown, a black, and an orange crayon and set them next to her paper. She was determined to draw a *real* giraffe, one that looked like a giraffe should, not like some dumb cartoon.

Two kids fought over a purple crayon next to her, but she ignored them and focused on the first curves of the giraffe's head until she heard her mother's voice beside her. "Have fun today. I got to go."

Jess mumbled a goodbye, but wasn't too concerned about it. This giraffe, though …

"Hi. I'm Sandra," came a small voice from beside her. "You want to be friends?"

Jess inspected the girl cautiously. Her dark brown hair was pulled back into two low pigtails held by pink bobble bands, and her squinty green eyes waited eagerly for a response.

"Yeah, okay." Jess went back to her drawing.

"My mother is the teacher," Sandra said.

"Neat."

"My father is a congressman."

The giraffe's neck was almost proportionate. Jess added just a little more length before drawing the body below it, starting with the chest. "I don't know what that means."

Apparently, Sandra didn't like that because she puffed up and huffed exasperatedly. When Jess turned to look at her, she noted that Sandra sort of resembled a giraffe with her chest stuck out like that and her neck extended as long as she could get it with her chin turned up like she was stretching to reach some good leaves. "It means he's the most important person in Mooretown."

Jessica knew that to be incorrect. Her mom had told her time and time again that *she*, Jess, was the most important person in this town. God had even agreed a handful of times.

Without meaning to, Jess chuckled.

Sandra threw her hands onto her hips. "What! You think he's not? What do *your* mom and dad do? Oh wait, your mom makes sales calls and you don't know who your dad is."

How does she know about Mom?

"I do know who my daddy is," Jess mumbled, hoping Sandra would stop being her friend and leave her alone.

"Oh yeah? Who then?"

"None of your business. He's in Heaven." There. That would be the end of it, just like Destinee had promised.

Only it wasn't. "Just because your dad is dead doesn't mean you don't have to say who he is. I bet your daddy was a criminal. I bet your parents weren't even married when they had you."

The other kids at the table had clued into the conversation and Jess could feel their eyes on her, waiting for her response. She hated how much that bothered her. With the stupid bright colors everywhere making her angry and with Sandra prodding, Jess couldn't focus enough on what a giraffe leg looked like, and she was about to ruin the whole drawing because of it.

"He's not a criminal." Why wouldn't Sandra just leave her alone?

"So you *do* know who he is."

"He's in Heaven." Jess doubted it would work any better this time around.

And she was right. "How do you know he's in Heaven? He could be … in the other place." She let the words linger in the air, and none of the other kids dared break the silence first.

Jess couldn't focus. Which way did the knee joints go on the hind legs? She couldn't recall the image while so much was going on.

"God!" she spat, breaking her mother's rule but hoping it would put an end to things. "God is my father!"

Sandra's squinty eyes popped open for a moment, then she quickly broke into laughter. Why was she pointing? Why was everyone laughing?

"You think *God* is your father?"

Jess had screwed up; she realized that. But then she remembered something she'd heard God say and thought maybe she could recover without lying. "We're all God's children …" Saying it with any real oomph was impossible, though, because it felt like she was giving away something she held dear, something that made her feel special.

She gritted her teeth and scribbled the brown crayon

over her giraffe's messed-up leg then eventually over the entire drawing as the kids continued to laugh.

"Stop it or I'll tell!" said a new voice next to her.

That put a swift end to the laughing.

Jess looked up to see who her savior was and saw a tiny wisp of a girl with long but delicate white-blonde hair that reflected the harsh fluorescent lights of the classroom in a soft, peaceful glow. The girl's crystal-blue eyes peered out from beneath dark lashes as she smiled at Jessica.

Sandra and her audience at the table stood up and ran off to destroy some kid's block tower, and Jess took a deep breath.

"Sorry they were being mean to you," said the little girl.

Jess didn't say anything and looked down at her scribbled drawing with regret.

"You can still start over," said the girl. "Maybe try something else this time."

Jess frowned. "Yeah, I guess so. I wanted to draw a giraffe, though."

"Can I draw with you?" the girl asked.

Jess nodded and the little girl sat.

"Are you my friend?" asked Jess.

The little girl grabbed two new sheets of paper and placed one carefully in front of Jess then one in front of herself. "Yes."

"What's your name?"

"Miranda."

"I'm Jessica."

"Okay, so now we're going to draw something and not talk while we do it."

Jessica liked the sound of that, and she liked Miranda. The girl felt more like a friend than Sandra had.

The problem now was inspiration. Starting all over with a giraffe didn't sound like fun, so what to draw, what to draw ...

She looked around the room and saw a tall, thin women breaking up bickering between Sandra and the kid who had built the now-destroyed block tower. As soon as Jess's eyes landed on the woman, an image flashed in her mind, one unlike anything Jess had ever seen before. Was that a memory? It felt like a memory, but it wasn't of anything she'd actually seen with her own eyes. The pretty, tall blonde was in the image, behaving in a way Jess couldn't explain. In fact, the entire scene made little sense to her, but at least it was vivid, so it was something to draw.

She closed her eyes and homed in on the image again to study the shapes. Then she began to draw, pouring all her focus into it. How much time passed, she didn't know. But finally, she felt like it was done. She sat back and looked at it. It was close enough to what she'd seen in her mind.

Miranda looked over. "What's that?"

Jess shrugged. "I don't know. Some people. What's yours?"

"A taco stand. They have them where my daddy lives."

Mrs. Thomas moved to the front of the classroom and clapped her hands three times. "When I do that, you clap three times and then stay silent for instruction. Understand? Okay. Let's try it."

THIS IS DUMB.

I don't know, I like clapping. Don't you have an earthquake to clean up?

WHY DON'T YOU LET ME WORRY ABOUT THAT.

Mrs. Thomas introduced herself and then introduced her teaching assistant, Ms. Rickles—the tall blonde woman in Jessica's picture. Even just a quick glance at Ms. Rickles's large watery eyes made it obvious that was sheer terror behind her plastered-on smile.

"Just like this is your first time being in kindergarten," Mrs. Thomas continued, "this is Ms. Rickles's first year as a teaching assistant, so she wants to come around and get to know each of you to start the school year. I'll be doing the same."

Jess decided to add a few finishing touches to her drawing to help impress the teachers when they made it around the room to where she and Miranda waited.

WHAT ARE YOU DRAW—OH ME. WHERE DID YOU COME UP WITH THAT?

I don't know, I just saw it.

DO YOU KNOW WHAT IT IS?

No. Just a woman and a man wrestling.

NAKED?

Yes. Is naked bad?

IT'S COMPLICATED.

Ms. Rickles skipped over Sandra's group and instead headed straight to the small table where Miranda and Jessica sat finishing up their art.

She started by asking for their names, complimenting their names, and then after that, Ms. Rickles looked at Miranda's drawing. "Would you tell me about your drawing?" She had a quivery singsong voice that made Jessica feel a little sorry for her.

Miranda pointed to each aspect as she explained. "That's a road and that's a rainbow and that's a taco stand and that's my daddy getting a taco."

"Wonderful! And what about you, Jessi— Oh good lord."

That wasn't the response Jess had hoped for. She felt her face heat up and knew that she was about to be in trouble, though she didn't really understand why.

"Um," Ms. Rickles said, keeping her posture rigid like Jess had only ever seen reptile experts do while confronting a particularly venomous snake, "what exactly is your drawing?"

Jessica looked up at her, confused. Didn't she know? "It's you." She pointed to the woman whose naked torso was draped facedown across the bed.

"I–I don't ..." Ms. Rickles's face flushed.

"And that's—" She pointed to the naked man standing behind Ms. Rickles, pressed up against her bottom half. It felt like she should know who it was, but she didn't have a name ...

MR. WURST.

"Mr. Wurst."

Ms. Rickles jumped up to standing like the snake had struck, then, in a much less singsongy and much more quivering voice, said, "How *dare* you! You— You have no idea what you're talking about! How— *How dare you!*"

"Huh?" asked Jess, slinking low in her tiny chair.

She was sure the whole class was looking at her, but she

was too scared to take her eyes off the teaching assistant long enough to check. She wanted to cry because she didn't mean to be bad. Could she even be bad? She'd never been bad before. She was the daughter of God, didn't that mean something?

Ms. Rickles's gaze darted down to the drawing on the page again just before Mrs. Thomas appeared behind her and grabbed her arm, causing the young woman to jump at the sudden contact. She turned to face Mrs. Thomas, who was scowling fiercely. "What exactly is going on here?"

Pointing a finger in Jess's face, Ms. Rickles stammered, "Sh—she's accusing me of … Her drawing! It's inappropriate and a lie!"

Mrs. Thomas remained calm, which was no small comfort to Jess. "May I see the drawing, Jessica?"

A pulsating heat rushed down from Jessica's face as she managed to lift her arm, which felt like lead, grab the picture, and hand it over to Mrs. Thomas.

The teacher examined it. "I see," she said, furrowing her brows. She looked up and faced Ms. Rickles. "And this woman is you? Not Mrs. Wurst?"

Jess thought she saw the faintest glimmer of a smile tilt the corner of Mrs. Thomas's mouth.

Ms. Rickles continued glaring down at Jess. "That's what *she's* saying!"

"Well, what do *you* say, Kira?" Mrs. Thomas's voice remained steady.

Ms. Rickles seemed to choke on words. Finally, she spat, "I think she has a lot of nerve making that sort of an accusation, considering *her* mother's reputation!"

The tenuous cord of patience in Mrs. Thomas's voice snapped. "That's enough." It came out like a slap, and Ms. Rickles took a quick step back. "She's *five*, Kira! You may not be that much older, but you're old enough to know better. I think you need to go take an early lunch."

"It's only nine thirty—"

Jess hoped Mrs. Thomas never looked at her the way she was looking at Ms. Rickles. "I *said* go take lunch. A long one. I'll let you know when your lunch is over, do you understand?"

Ms. Rickles burst into tears, grabbed her purse from behind the desk, and then sprinted out of the classroom without looking back.

Most of the class watched her go. Sandra didn't seem to think much of the interaction once she realized it wasn't Jess getting in trouble, and she continued ravaging the bookshelf.

Mrs. Thomas leaned down and whispered, "Don't worry, you're not in trouble," before folding the drawing into fourths and addressing the class to say that it was time for an early snack.

YOU SHOULDN'T HAVE DRAWN THAT.

Why did you tell me to, then?

I DIDN'T.

Then how did I see it?

I MUST HAVE LET MY GUARD DOWN AND YOU SAW A MEMORY.

You were thinking about that?

I WAS THINKING ABOUT MS. RICKLES'S SIN OF ADULTERY, YES. I'LL HAVE TO BE MORE CAREFUL NEXT

TIME TO NOT LET YOU SEE. THAT ONLY HAPPENED A COUPLE OF TIMES WITH YOUR BROTHER AND NOT UNTIL HE WAS MUCH OLDER.

Will you smite Ms. Rickles?

FOR ADULTERY? NO. THERE ARE A FEW OTHER THINGS I'D LIKE TO DO TO HER, THOUGH …

Jess wondered what those things might be, but God made so many strange comments that she'd decided long ago not to linger on them all. She'd also heard from more than one person that God worked in mysterious ways, so she usually didn't worry about it.

Once Mrs. Thomas had finished sprinkling the Goldfish crackers onto each student's napkin, she pulled Jess aside to sit with her in a beanbag chair corner, where she unfolded the drawing and held it out for Jess to look at with her.

"You're not in trouble, Jess. I just want to hear from you what it is that you drew."

Jess pointed to each thing as she explained. "That's Ms. Rickles and that's Mr. Wurst. I don't know who Mr. Wurst is, though."

"That's okay. I do. And who's that grinning face in the corner?"

Jess looked at it. She hadn't remembered drawing that, but she knew immediately who it was. "That's God. He's watching them sin."

Mrs. Thomas held back a smile, though Jess didn't know what was worth smiling about. "I see. And why did you draw this?"

She shrugged. "I just saw a picture of it in my head and

I drew it. I messed up my giraffe, so I didn't know what else to draw."

Mrs. Thomas reached out and rubbed Jessica's back comfortingly. "Okay. That's all I was curious about. If you want, I can hold onto this for you and we don't have to talk about it anymore, not even with your mom."

While she didn't suspect Destinee would care one way or another about the drawing, since it was God's fault and Jess could simply tell her that, she appreciated Mrs. Thomas's offer anyway. Maybe she'd misjudged Mrs. Thomas at the start of the day. Mrs. Thomas actually seemed nice. Even at such a young age, Jessica could recognize a protector when she saw one, and Mrs. Thomas certainly seemed to fit the bill.

Not even Sandra messed with Jess for the rest of the day, allowing her and Miranda to keep to themselves and become even better friends as they bonded over favorite colors (purple and green), favorite foods (cheese pizza and Sonic Blasts), and favorite new friends (each other). And when she showed up the next morning and the morning after that, Ms. Rickles was nowhere to be found, and Jessica suspected that kindergarten might turn out to be the funnest thing she ever did.

Chapter Three

The first week of school flew by, and Jess had never imagined life could be so eventful. Every day so far she and Miranda had come up with a new game to play, and every day students in her class had done something they weren't supposed to do that was funny to watch and got them in trouble with Mrs. Thomas.

God had been uncharacteristically quiet all week, too, which might have also explained why Jess considered this the best week of her life.

And it was only Friday morning.

The first class of the day, after story time, was science. The lesson had been on landforms like continents and oceans and deserts and mountains. Jess's mind snapped to attention when Mrs. Thomas mentioned the Himalayas.

She raised her hand and was called on. "Was there an earthquake there recently?"

Mrs. Thomas smiled and nodded. "Yes! Very good!" She looked out over the tiny faces seated on the rug around her chair as she continued to hold open the book to the page on mountains. "Does anyone else know what an earthquake is?"

Jess felt pride radiate through her. But she was also relieved that God hadn't been lying about the earthquake as an excuse to disappear. It seemed strange that He would lie, anyway. *Could* God lie? Jess was just glad to hear about what the Himalayas were and to see pictures of them in the science book. She decided that she wanted to visit there someday, but only if God promised there wouldn't be an earthquake, because those seemed scary.

After science was recess. It was the only time of day besides lunch when Mrs. Thomas's class got to interact with Mrs. Gregory's kindergarten class, as well as a first grade and a second-grade class. That didn't mean Jess had much interest in playing with the other kids. Why would she, when they just wanted to run and climb on the white-hot metal of the playscape and monkey bars rather than do the sensible thing and play in the sandbox, which was shaded from the late-August sun by the shadow of the school? A small group of first graders were the only other students that opted for the large sandbox alongside Jess and Miranda, who had set their minds to the mammoth task of re-creating the Himalayas as accurately as their memory allowed. The mountain range had only been covered briefly in the lesson, but Jess knew enough about it now to know there at least had to be an Everest. So while Jess focused her energy on that, filling a small plastic bucket with water from the faucet (with permission and assistance from Mrs. Thomas, obviously) to moisten the sand enough so that it stuck together, allowing for steeper inclines, Miranda set out to construct the smaller mountains of which they didn't know the names. Once Jess was finished with Everest, Miranda squiggled her finger around the peak to give it the appearance of being snowcapped and they both giggled.

Then out of nowhere, a rock the size of a silver dollar came flying in and narrowly missed knocking over Everest, landing instead in the flat sand a few feet behind where Jess knelt.

"Hey!" She looked up to see where the rock had come from. A blond boy with golden skin and freckles stood holding his stomach and laughing his head off.

"Stop that!" She'd seen the boy around at recess, but he was in the other kindergarten class, so she didn't know his name.

He picked up a bigger rock and threw it at their mountains, and this time it hit one of the lesser peaks and blasted it away.

"I said stop!" Jess insisted, getting to her feet. Why wouldn't he listen? Why was he being mean?

Another projectile came flying in, and Jess's relief that it'd missed the Himalayas was short-lived when the rock found her shin bone instead. She yelped and felt rage surge through her like she'd never felt before. "You hit me!" It didn't make sense why he was so set on being mean. She wanted to force him to stop, but she didn't know how.

Miranda stood. "Christopher Riley!" She put her hands on her hips. "I'm going to tell the teacher on you if you do that again!"

He paused for a moment, seemed to consider the threat, then grabbed another rock from the playground gravel and threw it, finally hitting Everest toward the middle and causing the quickly drying top half to crumble. He braced himself on one of the metal posts of the playscape as he cackled maniacally.

"Nooo! Stop it, stop it, *stop it!*" Jess yelled, clenching her fists and stomping a foot hard in the sand. Her whole body felt like it was on fire with anger and ... something else that she was only vaguely aware of and had no name for.

Her wrath seemed to amuse Christopher, and he kept laughing, only now he was pointing at her while he did, which was worse for some reason. An older girl—perhaps even in second grade—paused in her game of tag to stare from Christopher to Jessica, undoubtedly trying to figure out what was so funny. Two more older kids paused nearby, too, and now that the torment had an audience, it felt even worse than ever. She could hear Miranda scolding Christopher, but her brain seemed unable to make out the words through the high-pitched buzzing that had begun in her ears.

Jess's eyes flickered up to a grackle perched atop the blue metal pole that Christopher was using to hold himself up as he doubled over in laughter. The bird stared directly at her.

Even the bird is laughing at me!

It was too much, and before Jess could understand a fraction of what was happening, a swell of heat rushed through her and tugged free of her body in one strong burst.

The grackle's squawk was cut short by a sickening popping sound after the bird rapidly inflated like a balloon hooked up to an automatic tire pump then exploded in a puff of feathers that launched hollow bone shards and viscera in all directions. Nothing within a five-foot radius of it was spared from the gore, as blood and guts splattered onto Christopher's hair and cheek, stained the white stripes on his polo shirt, and caused similar damage to the other kids who'd gathered round to watch the spectacle. Jess and Miranda, at least, were far enough away to avoid the mess, but that didn't make the sight of it any less brutal.

All movement within earshot of the squawk ceased, and Jess froze, wide-eyed, knowing with certainty that she was responsible for the bird's gruesome end.

Then the crying started—a chorus of voices that was finally enough of a variation from the playful screaming to draw the teachers' attention. Mrs. Thomas and Mrs. Gregory ran over toward the source of the cacophony, and Jess decided it was best if she turned back to her Himalayas and pretended to have no part in the situation. Miranda looked at her strangely for a moment and then followed her lead, and they silently set out to rebuild Everest.

"Oh Jesus!" Mrs. Gregory exclaimed, and Jess knew the teacher had finally noticed all the blood. It would be impossible not to. Who knew one stupid grackle could contain so much mess?

Jess tried not to listen to the commotion behind her,

but that was difficult when there was nothing else to listen to.

"What *happened?*" Mrs. Thomas asked one of the nearby kids, not sounding angry so much as disgusted.

Luckily, most of the crying children seemed too distraught to actually say that a grackle blew up for no reason.

Crouched next to Jess rather than across from her, where she would have been able to see the crime scene laid out, Miranda leaned close and asked quietly, "Are you really the daughter of God?"

Jess nodded. "Yeah. Do you believe me?"

Miranda drew snow tops on one of the newly rebuilt mountains. "Yes. Did you blow up that bird?"

"I didn't mean to. I've never done that before."

"Okay," Miranda replied softly as she packed some of the sand together at the base of a mountain.

"And I *smote* it. I think that's the word God uses."

Miranda giggled. "That's a silly word."

Despite herself, Jess giggled too. "Yeah. I know."

"Why did you smote it?"

"I didn't mean to."

"Did you mean to smote Christopher Riley instead?"

Jess had to think about that. She would never have wanted to do to Christopher what she did to the bird. In fact, she didn't even want to do to the bird what she did to the bird. "No. I just wanted him to stop. I didn't know I could do that."

"That's good. Can I tell you a super secret?"

Jess was bad at secrets. God had told her as much before. "I'm not good at keeping secrets."

"Can I tell you anyway?"

"If you want to."

Miranda leaned in and used a flat hand to direct the whispers straight into Jess's ear. "I think Christopher is cute."

She assumed Miranda was referring to the version of Christopher that wasn't covered in giblets and goo and nodded as she waited patiently for the super secret. But Miranda didn't continue. "What's the secret?"

Miranda frowned and blinked quickly, staring thoughtfully at Jess like she was missing something. "That's it. Don't tell anyone."

Ever since Jess had first understood language, the words "don't tell anyone" had usually been accompanied by more serious things than thinking something was cute.

From her mother it was, "Don't tell anyone that you talk to God."

From her grandma it was, "Don't tell anyone how much of a slut your mother is."

From God it was, DON'T TELL ANYONE, BUT I WASN'T REALLY PAYING ATTENTION WHEN I CREATED AUSTRALIA.

But to think a boy was cute? Jess thought plenty of things were cute. She thought bunnies were cute. She thought baby giraffes were cute. She might even have thought that grackle was a little cute before it was nothing but guts and feathers. She supposed boys could be cute, too.

"I don't understand why you don't want me to tell people that you think Christopher is cute."

Miranda looked at her like, *come on,* opening her eyes wide and tilting her head to the side. "Because I don't want anyone to know I have a crush on a boy!"

Oh. Wait. That sounded familiar. "You have a crush on him?" She crinkled her nose. "What does that mean?"

"It means I want to kiss him," Miranda said, and then she cupped her hands over her mouth and giggled.

"Ew. That's gross." Jess looked back over at Christopher, who was still covered in bird mush but had finally stopped crying. She imagined kissing him, sans grackle bits, and the idea wasn't *terrible* ...

Then Mrs. Thomas turned Christopher to face them and gave him a gentle shove forward. His shoulders slumped and his head sagged as he approached them in the sandbox.

"Sorry I threw rocks at your sand mountains." He looked like he was about to start crying again.

"That's okay." Jess wanted to add that she was sorry she smote the bird, but she decided against it.

"You shouldn't make her mad, you know," Miranda said, her hands on her hips. "Her father is God. She's got magical powers. God powers."

"Miranda!" Jess couldn't believe what her friend had just said.

Christopher's bloodshot eyes popped open and he took a small step back. "What?" He studied Miranda then turned to look at Jess. "You're God's daughter?"

For a moment, it was clear he was actually considering it, maybe even awed by the notion. But then his face changed, and he burst out laughing again. "You think God is your father!"

Jess's eyes darted around to the faces that might have heard what Christopher had just shouted. A few of the other children looked puzzled, Mrs. Gregory seemed concerned, but Mrs. Thomas simply appeared amused.

Jess felt her face turn red, and she shut her eyes to calm herself so that she didn't smite something else. Maybe if she just didn't say anything, everyone would go away.

But the opposite of that happened, and the worst possible person decided to show up on scene: Trent. He wasn't even in Jess's class, but she knew this cocky, snub-nosed, freckle-faced boy's name due to the fact that every teacher and even some of the students chastised him constantly. His face reminded Jess of her neighbor's horrid Pekingese that never stopped yapping.

Trent went to stand by Christopher and similarly pointed and laughed at Jess. "God doesn't have a daughter!" he said. "He only has a son! Anyone who thinks different is going to Hell, so there! Plus, girls stink!"

"Trent!" Mrs. Thomas scolded.

Miranda reached out, grabbed a fistful of sand, and hurled it at the boy. "You don't know anything, Trent! Go away!"

"Miranda!" Mrs. Gregory scolded.

Trent laughed defiantly then shouted, *"Earthquake!"* and began stomping out the Himalayas one by one before Mrs. Thomas was able to run over, scoop him up under the armpits, and carry him out of the sandbox.

But the damage was already done, and Trent cackled in satisfaction. "What? It was an earthquake."

Mrs. Thomas began giving him an earful, and when Jess looked at Christopher, he was staring at her in terror. Was he worried she'd smite another bird, or worse? So maybe he did believe her after all. And if so, he was right to worry, because she felt heat inside her about to boil over, and it was all aimed squarely now at Trent.

Mrs. Gregory looked at her watch, inhaled deeply and mouthed *thank you* to the sky before announcing that recess was over and it was time for everyone to head inside.

"Except you two," came Mrs. Thomas's voice from behind Jess. She turned slowly, worried she'd somehow managed to upset her favorite teacher, only to realize that Mrs. Thomas wasn't talking to her or Miranda; she was, of course, talking to Christopher and Trent.

Christopher, at least, had the decency to slink over, shoulders hunched. Jess almost felt sorry for him when he walked like that, still covered in grackle bits. But she didn't feel bad for Trent—not even a little—who bounced around with a stupid grin and had the nerve to repeat back everything Mrs. Thomas was trying to say to him.

Mrs. Thomas's patience grew as thin as her lips, which curled into two tight lines just below her flared nostrils, and Jess knew that if her teacher had been able to smite Trent in that moment, she definitely would have.

Turning her back on them, Jessica jogged to catch up with Miranda, who was already headed toward the cool AC.

"I hate Trent," she vented.

Miranda nodded. "At least Courtney was out sick today."

Courtney was Trent's prissy twin sister, and while she was in Mrs. Gregory's kindergarten class and therefore had recess with Mrs. Thomas's class every day, Jess had yet to actually talk to the little girl, who clearly thought she was too good to relate to the likes of Jess and Miranda. But Jess would take snobbery over Trent's abrasive bullying any day.

"Yeah, they're both the worst."

Miranda giggled. "That's a funny joke."

They crossed over into the cool air of the kindergarten hallway and Jess pushed her sweaty hair from her face. "No. I'm serious. They're the worst kids in kindergarten, maybe even the whole school."

"Ohhh ... I thought you meant because of their last name."

Jess shook her head, feeling like she was missing something. Because she was.

"Courtney and Trent," Miranda filled in. "Their last name is Wurst, so I just thought ... I thought you knew that when you drew the picture of their dad."

Jess shook her head before Mrs. Gregory lined up both kindergarten classes against opposite walls and asked them to be silent.

So Trent's dad was a sinner, huh? She'd have to keep that in mind next time the stupid bully tried to pick on her. She didn't quite understand what being a sinner meant, but she knew saying it to Trent might shut him up, which was all she could ask for.

Mrs. Thomas appeared, hurrying down the hallway

from the direction of the principal's office with a much pleasanter expression than Jess had last seen her wearing. She spoke quietly to Mrs. Gregory, who nodded, and then the teachers each led their classes back into the classrooms to start the day's math lesson.

It wasn't until after school let out that Jess spotted Christopher and Trent again, and she was satisfied to discover that Trent's stupid grin was nowhere to be seen. Instead, he and Christopher both sat on the steps of the school, shoulder to shoulder, sulking quietly as they waited for their parents to pick them up.

Trent's ride arrived first, and when he got up to leave, Mrs. Thomas waved to the woman in the minivan— presumably Mrs. Wurst—and hollered, "Hey, Trent." He turned to look at her, his eyes brimming with a fear that Jess hadn't expected to see in such a cocky little brat. Mrs. Thomas simply smiled at him and added, "Don't forget what I told you." Trent's eyes went even wider, and he nodded frantically before practically leaping into the backseat of the minivan and slamming the door behind him.

Jess turned to Miranda, who was struggling futilely to braid a chunk of her blonde hair, and said, "I hope I never make Mrs. Thomas angry."

Miranda gave up and let go of the strands, which she swept back from her face. "No way. Mrs. Thomas loves you. I don't think there's anything you could do that would make her be angry with you."

It had only been a week, but it did seem that way. Questions started to form in Jessica's mind that she felt too embarrassed to speak aloud. Did Mrs. Thomas believe Jess was God's daughter? Was that why she seemed to like Jess so much? She desperately wanted to be liked by Mrs. Thomas, so maybe she should stop asking questions and just appreciate how things were.

Chapter Four

8 AGC

It was a dream come true. Jess was only in third grade, but she wasn't sure how life could get better from here. Her fingertips gripped the chain-link fence that stood between her and the two giraffes—a mother and calf grazing from a tall bush, serene despite the hellscape of an enclosure where they spent their lives—and she pressed her face against the metal so hard that when she pulled away, two red diamond-shaped imprints framed her eyes.

This field trip, orchestrated by Mrs. Thomas, was even better than Jess had dreamed it might be. It was like her third-grade teacher had planned it especially for her, though obviously that wasn't the case. But part of her pretended it was.

"Giraffes are awesome!" said Christopher Riley from beside her.

She wanted to tell him no duh, but when she was only

twenty feet from her favorite animal, it was impossible for her to reply with anything but an awed, "Yeah ..."

"It's like they have little antennas," Chris said earnestly, pressing his face against the chain-link almost as enthusiastically as Jess was.

"They're called ossicones," she informed him, "and the males use them to fight."

"Why do giraffes have such long necks?" said a shrill, nasally voice from the other side of her. Jess shuddered at the sound. Luke McAllister. She wanted so badly to be mean to her pale, gangly, sour-breathed classmate so he'd leave her alone and let her enjoy this special moment, but she didn't for two reasons. The first was that she wasn't good at being mean and usually just made herself look stupid when she tried it, and the second was that Luke's uncle, Randy, had been assigned as the field trip chaperone for their small group, which consisted of her, Christopher, Luke, and Courtney Wurst.

"They have long necks, *Luke*"—she stressed his name, hoping he might pick up on how stupid he was—"so they can eat leaves that no other animal can reach."

"Nope," said Luke.

"Yes," Jess replied, pulling her eyes away from the beautiful beasts to look at the twerp who was ruining everything.

"Nope," repeated Luke, wearing a dumb grin on his stupid face. "They have long necks so they don't have to smell their stinky feet!" He cackled at his own joke, and then turned to the enclosure, grabbed the fence, and began rattling it and hollering, "Hey giraffes!" over and over again, like they might actually understand English.

The jarring noise caused the calf to scamper behind its mother so that Jess could only see it from the middle of the neck down.

"You're an idiot," Christopher said to Luke.

Jess agreed wholeheartedly, though she refrained from saying it.

When Luke cackled again and continued shaking the fence, Christopher hopped around Jess and shoved Luke hard, catching him by surprise and sending him flying.

Luke only just managed to get his feet under him enough to keep from tumbling onto his stupid bony butt.

"Quit being a punk," Christopher said.

Once Luke's shock lifted, he turned tail and ran over to the bench where Randy sat, to tattle to his uncle.

Christopher didn't seem concerned and returned his gaze to the giraffes. "I hate Luke. He's so annoying. I can't believe I had to sit next to him on the bus."

"That stinks."

"You have no idea. You got to sit next to Miranda."

Even still, the drive from Mooretown to the Dallas Zoo had felt like forever. But if she'd been stuck next to Luke, or anyone other than her best friend, really, the drive might have become unbearable.

"Why didn't you sit next to Trent?" she asked.

"He wanted to sit next to his stupid sister."

Jess couldn't imagine why anyone would want to sit next to Courtney Wurst. Trent spent most of his time as a nightmarish blur, but at least you knew what he was thinking because he never stopped shouting it. Courtney, though, while slower moving and quieter than her twin, never lowered her snub nose from the air and preferred to hold her tongue until she was able to accurately identify whatever a person was feeling most insecure about at that moment at which point she would unleash a perfectly executed jab at said insecurity. Jess had never met anyone so talented at being cruel and getting away with it.

"Where is she anyway?" Jess pulled her eyes away from the giraffes to search for their errant group member and spotted her sitting on the bench next to Randy—*not* Mr. McAllister, but *Randy*; he'd corrected them on that right away when he'd introduced himself earlier that morning.

So Courtney was still sulking, was she? And all over some stupid argument about Noah's ark? Jess probably shouldn't have contradicted her when she got going on it, but the things Courtney had said just didn't make any sense. The flaws in her arguments seemed so obvious, even without God's commentary on how it actually went down and His bemoaning of how a good scribe is hard to find.

A merciful tour guide had put an end to the argument by backing up Jess on the whole evolution thing until Courtney huffed, said it was their eternal damnation at stake, not hers, and took to calling the Dallas Zoo the "Devil's menagerie" as often as she could.

Jessica was grateful for the tour guide's support on the matter, but it would've been even better if God spoke directly to people other than Jessica to settle arguments. Instead, she was forced to be the intermediary, stuck in a game of divine telephone that no one else was keen to play.

While she had no formal religious education (outside of God's occasional "fun facts"), it was impossible to grow up without bits of Biblical lore filtering down to her. She could piece together most of the stories—of Noah, Jesus, Moses —from snippets and allusions made by her more openly religious classmates like the Wursts, Christopher Riley, and the massive Smith family, who had six kids attending Mooreson Elementary alone with four more distributed between Marymoore Junior High and Mooremont High School.

Through social osmosis, Jessica knew Jesus liked to fish, wore sandals, and died for her sins. However, she didn't know what it meant to die for someone's sins. Was he wrongly accused of something? Perhaps even framed? That part was unclear. But what *was* clear to her was that his death had been gruesome and she ought to be ashamed of herself because of that. Oh, and Jesus was her half-brother, apparently.

Moses was a little more mysterious. All she knew about him was that he parted a sea. And he wandered the desert with Jews. She never understood why he had so many Jewish friends until she met a boy named David at the public park one day when she was seven years old. David played safari with her for an hour and a half before his mother took him home. David was Jewish. At least that's what he'd told her when she confessed to him that she was God's daughter.

"Like Jesus?" David had said.

Jessica nodded tentatively. "I guess."

"Oh."

"Can we still play safari?"

"Sure. I don't believe in Jesus."

That was a first. "You don't?"

"No. I'm a Jew."

Her mind had immediately concocted this string of logic: people who believed in Jesus included Courtney and Trent, and they were horrible. People who didn't believe in Jesus included David, and he knew that lionesses, rather than the lions, were actually the neatest members of the pride.

If she had to wander the desert for a long time, she would much prefer the company of Jews than Wursts. Moses had chosen well.

Noah, on the other hand, was a figure she'd gleaned little about from her cohort and too much about from dear old Dad.

From the kids at school, she'd learned: Noah built a boat called an ark to survive a massive flood. He'd gathered his family plus two of every animal onto the ark to survive the flood, and afterward, everything on the ark became either a mommy or daddy of everything on earth today.

There were some obvious holes in that story that sank it right into the biblical floodwaters, so far as Jessica was concerned.

But God had stepped in and, rather than plugging up the holes with detail and further explanation, presented her a brand new story that was the aircraft carrier of arks—expansive, clunky, with too many small parts—and went like this: folks in the known biblical world were getting a little complacent and neurotic. When God couldn't gently nudge them to branch out (figuratively and genealogically), meet various indigenous people, and triangulate new wisdom from other cultures, He decided to take a more forceful approach.

NOAH'S JOB WAS TO TELL EVERYONE ABOUT THE FLOOD SO THEY WOULD VACATE THE AREA. INSTEAD, HE USED THE KNOWLEDGE TO BRAG ABOUT BEING THE CHOSEN ONE.

This was a common theme in God's stories.

I TOLD HIM TO LEAVE, BUT HE WOULDN'T LISTEN. HE ASKED WHAT HIS OPTIONS WERE. I SAID, "SET OUT AND FIND HIGHER GROUND OR, OH, I DUNNO, BUILD A BIG OL' BOAT, I GUESS."

God's sarcasm was lost on Noah, whose critical thinking had been slightly stunted by a swift donkey hoof to the head as a child, and he decided building an ark was an easy way to show off to everyone that God had spoken only to *him* and no one else.

IT IS WHERE THE TERM "SHOWBOAT" COMES FROM.

Really?

YES. BUT IT WOULD BE MANY MORE YEARS BEFORE I INTRODUCED THE TERM TO MANKIND. I JUST SORTA SAT ON IT FOR MILLENIA.

To corroborate his own story, Noah began rounding up animals, a mating pair of each kind. Or at least he'd intended to get two of every animal. However, animals don't have the hubris of man, and because of that, they tend to be the first to flee when all signs point to natural disaster. They don't try to build boats or dikes or bunkers. When they sense impending threat, they run the hell away.

For that reason, Noah's animal harvesting yielded little fruit. And what fruit it did yield was old or sickly, unable to leave with the rest of its kind.

By the end of the flood, thanks to the short food supply on the ark, there was generally only one of every apex predator left. Those were the only ones that had stood a chance.

As Noah and his wife Norma wandered off the ark after the flood, they feasted upon the animals that remained, and it was a small comfort amid their huge mistake that at least they could overpower a lion with stage-three lung cancer (they didn't know he had cancer; only God knew.)

Jessica hadn't explained all of this to Courtney, though. Instead, she'd presented an abridged argument that focused on inbreeding and the food chain.

In the end, Courtney had stomped off to stand by Randy, her nose in the air.

But Jess knew better than to think that was the end of it with her. Retribution would be swift, though Jessica was pretty sure it wouldn't come until after they'd left the zoo.

She might as well enjoy her day. Besides, Randy didn't seem to mind having Courtney sulk next to him as they visited each exhibit on Jess's must-see list.

Luke tried his best to tattle on Christopher, but Randy merely smiled placidly at his nephew, and even from ten yards away, Jess could tell Randy wasn't actually listening.

She sighed. "I wish I could have been in Mrs. Thomas's group." She turned back toward the giraffes.

"Me too," said Christopher. "And she doesn't even like

me. Anyone would be better than Luke and his weird, lumpy uncle."

It was such an apt description that Jess had to laugh. Randy wasn't fat, and he wasn't necessarily thin. Lumpy was a good word for it. Maybe *soft* too. It was like he stored most of his body fat in a doughy ring around his middle that sagged over his belt, straining against his tucked-in heather green polo shirt. The remainder of his fat was stored in two saggy lumps on his chest that reminded Jess of a pregnant gorilla's teats.

"What's next?" Christopher asked.

As much as she wanted to sit and watch the giraffes all day, she knew she'd regret it if she didn't see all the animals on the list she'd spent the previous week compiling.

She pulled the piece of notebook paper out of her pocket and began unfolding it when Christopher shouted, "Hey look! There's Trent and Mrs. Thomas! And they have frozen lemonade! No fair!"

He ran over to the other group.

Jess looked over her list. The lions' den was the next item down.

It was three o'clock. They'd already spent five hours at the zoo, and Jess could tell her classmates were growing bored. She was exhausted, too, but who knew when her next chance to visit the zoo would be.

She did, however, want to fill in Miranda on how annoying Luke was being and why Courtney was throwing a fit, so she followed Christopher over to where the two small groups had merged into one jumble by a tall map of the zoo.

Before she could get a word out, though, Miranda had important information to report.

"Mrs. Thomas is going to buy us ice cream after we finish our lemonade!" Miranda gulped her drink down hurriedly and then grimaced against the brain freeze. She held out the drink to Jess, who grabbed it and took a sip before handing it back to her best friend.

"Stupid Randy hasn't bought us anything," Jess said, careful not to be overheard by someone who might rat her out.

Christopher popped up next to her and tapped her on the arm with the back of his hand. "You hear that, Jess?"

"No, what?"

"Mrs. Thomas said our group can go with hers to get ice cream!"

Jess forced a smile. "Oh cool!" But now she was left with the decision of ice cream or lions.

"You don't seem excited," Christopher said, looking horrified.

"I just want to see the lions, is all."

A man's voice from behind her said, "Oh, I love lions." Jess turned toward the source to find Randy hovering behind her. "I'd like to see them, too," he added. Then he raised his voice to address the rest of the combined groups. "How about this, everyone. If you want to go see the lions, come with me, and if you want to get ice cream, go with Mrs. Thomas." He looked up at Mrs. Thomas for approval, and she shrugged and nodded.

"That works," she said.

But whether it was because everyone had started ignoring Randy or because ice cream had a tastier payoff than staring at lions, no one else responded to his offer, which left Jess the odd girl out.

Randy looked questioningly at Mrs. Thomas, who said, "I can handle them, no problem." Then she stepped through the crowd and leaned close to Jess, saying, "I tell you what, you go enjoy the lions for a while and I'll take the rest of the group over there to meet you and bring you some ice cream." She smiled and raised her eyebrows inquisitively. "That work?"

"Yeah! Thanks, Mrs. Thomas!"

The teacher winked then pressed a furtive finger to her lips before turning back toward the other students, and herding them in the direction of ice cream.

"Great! Shall we?" Randy asked. He sounded almost as excited as Jess felt.

"Yep!"

Jess took three steps in the direction of the lions before she felt that familiar voice booming inside her skull.

DON'T GO WITH HIM.

But I want to see the lions.

I'M TELLING YOU NOT TO GO WITH HIM.

And I'm telling you I'm going with him.

WHA— ARE YOU DISOBEYING ME?

I guess so.

THOU SHALT NOT GO WITH HIM!

I'm not sure what "shalt" means.

Randy held out a crooked elbow toward Jess. Was she

supposed to take it? She didn't want to, but he moved it closer to her.

DON'T TAKE HIS ARM.

But it would be rude not to. *He's lame, but he's trying to be nice.*

PEOPLE ACT NICE FOR A LOT OF REASONS.

I'll look like a jerk if I say no. He might even get mad and not take me to the lions. She didn't know Randy well at all, but if he was anything like his nephew, he was the type to throw a tantrum or lash out if he didn't get his way.

So she grabbed his crooked arm at the elbow, unable to keep from grimacing when the close proximity to him yielded a strong smell of cologne and sweat, and he led her toward the lions' den. She threw one look over her shoulder to where her classmates headed in the opposite direction and for a moment reconsidered how much she actually wanted to see the lions.

But she tamped down that feeling and continued along the path and around a corner with Randy, behind tall bushes and out of sight of the others.

"That's a pretty shirt you're wearing," Randy said, staring down at her.

How was she supposed to respond to that? It was just a shirt with an elephant face on it. "Thanks."

He jumped in front of her, halting her progress, and grinned. "You're very welcome. I love elephants. You know what I love most about elephants?"

Jess faked an itch on her shoulder so she could pull her arm free of his to scratch it. "No."

"Their silly trunks!" He reached down and traced his

finger over the elephant's trunk on her shirt, tickling her chest and stomach as he did so. She giggled involuntarily and jumped away. Randy laughed, too, showing off his yellow teeth and receding gums.

OH FOR MY SAKE. DAUGHTER, I COMMAND YOU TO RETURN TO YOUR GROUP.

No.

THOU SHALT—

Make me!

I CAN'T.

You can't? I thought you could do anything.

I MEAN, OF COURSE I CAN! I JUST DON'T WANT TO MAKE YOU. AND TRUST ME, YOU DON'T WANT ME TO MAKE YOU.

You're being weird.

"You all right there, Jennifer?" Randy asked, still leaning over in front of her, his hands braced on his knees. His attention shifted from her to a mother and son who strolled by.

She'd zoned out again, clearly. And Randy had noticed.

"Jessica," she corrected.

Once she spoke, he seemed much less concerned and stood up straight again. "That's what I said."

"No, it's not," she replied. "You called me Jennifer."

He flashed a forced grin. "Nope, you're wrong. Doesn't matter though."

He placed a hand flat between her shoulder blades and guided her onward. She wished he wouldn't touch her, so she quickened her steps to outpace his hand.

As they arrived at the observation area, separated from

the lions by only a sheet of thick glass, Jess decided that it was totally worth braving Randy's awkwardness to get this close to an alpha predator.

One of the lionesses lay right near the glass, staring passively at the observers on the other side. Jess thought there was something pitiful about the cat, something that made her wish there were no glass there at all, even though that probably wouldn't work out well for any of the humans involved.

Randy crouched down next to her, staring at the lioness as well. "I think I know where we can get a better look at the lions," he said in a low, mischievous tone, like some other adult might overhear and get upset. Did Randy know he was an adult? He was ancient—perhaps even in his thirties—and already had a large bald patch in his wispy strawberry-blond hair, but Jess felt like maybe no one had ever told him that he was grown up.

"I can see them pretty well from here," she said, pointing to the lioness only a few feet from her.

"Yeah, but she's just *lion* around." He stared at Jess expectantly, and finally, she gave in and chuckled at his lame joke so that he wouldn't be mad. "Don't you want to see them be more active?"

She did. But whatever he had in mind sounded like it might be against the rules. "I guess. But this is okay, too."

"Oh come on, you're not scared of breaking a few rules, are you?" He said it with a big goofy grin, and Jess finally felt too sorry for him to refuse.

"Okay."

NO. DO NOT LISTEN TO HIM. THOU SHALT NOT—

I will if I want to.

She wasn't sure which was more irritating, Randy's wimpiness or God's bossiness.

"This way," Randy said, and he led her around the enclosure to a set of roped-off stairs.

The stairs were walled in on either side by cement made to look like ruddy boulders. Jess paused. A yellow sign in plain view had *Trained Zoo Personnel Only* in large black letters.

Randy followed her gaze. "Don't worry. We'll just go up there really quick. No one has to know."

When she didn't proceed right away, he placed his hand between her shoulder blades again, and that got her moving.

Once they reached the top, they found themselves in a cove of sorts that overlooked the enclosure. With the fake rock walls surrounding them on all sides except the one that looked out over the lions' den, Jess was able to imagine there were no other visitors around, that she was on a solo safari in the wild, and it was just her and the lions.

Well, and Randy.

She approached the opening, which was blocked off with a chain-link gate. Beyond the gate was a drop of at least twenty feet into the enclosure, and Jess's nerves wouldn't allow her to lean against this fence like she had the one at the giraffes, for fear—albeit probably an illogical one—of the gate giving out against her weight, causing her to plummet off the platform.

Stop it, she coached herself. She was letting her

imagination run away with her and it was ruining what should be a tranquil experience. So she stood a foot back from the gate and kept a hand on the fake rock to stay planted in space.

With the warm afternoon sun unable to reach her above the ruddy cement walls, the chill of the early November weather quickly began to bite at Jess's ears and fingers. She removed her hand from the wall without thinking about it so she could rub her palms together as she looked down at a pair of cubs roughhousing near a small artificial pond.

"Are you cold?" Randy asked.

"Huh?"

"Here." He stepped between her and the gate, blocking her view of the cubs as he squatted down to be on eye level. He took her chilly hands in his. "Let me warm them up."

"Um." Neck hair bristled at the base of her skull. This wasn't right. Jess knew that immediately. She didn't know exactly how it was wrong, just that it felt *not right*. Randy was staring into her eyes in a way that adults never did.

"Your ears look chilly, too. Here." He reached up, placed a hand on either side of her head and began massaging her lobes.

That was too much. She pulled her head away and took a step back.

"What, are you scared of me?" Randy stayed crouched on his heels and motioned her back toward him. "Come on, Jennifer. I'm just trying to be nice. Nobody likes rude girls. If you ever want to have a boyfriend someday, you should learn how to relate to men."

Boyfriend? Why was he talking about boyfriends? That seemed to come out of nowhere.

When Jess took another small step away from him, he huffed impatiently and began to stand.

OH FOR THE LOVE OF ME.

Before Randy was totally upright, he stumbled back, almost like he'd been pushed. His eyes jolted wide with shock, and he scrambled to get his feet back under him. His back hit the gate, and the time between when the chain-link began to strain against his force and when it finally gave out seemed to stretch on forever.

Jess either couldn't or didn't want to move her feet— even long afterward she wasn't sure which was the case. All she could do was watch Randy's terrified expression disappear from view as he toppled over the edge and fell twenty feet into the lions' den. His yell was abruptly cut off by a hard *thunk*.

I should go get help.

DON'T BOTHER.

Jess took a few hesitant steps toward the edge, braced herself on the fake rock and looked down to find Randy in a cloud of dust, rolling slowly onto his side, trying to sit up. He moaned against his injuries from the fall, and when he looked back up and saw Jess staring down at him silently, he shouted. "Don't just stand there, you worthless little tease! Go get help."

It didn't seem real. She nodded slowly at him but didn't move. She was only *faintly* aware of the few onlookers who'd noticed that there was a man in the enclosure and were beginning to holler and point. But she was *acutely* aware of the lions who had taken notice and were stalking slowly toward him. Jess had seen lions act like that on television programs and she knew what was coming.

The lioness who had been *"lion* around*"* only minutes before was leading the hunt, and part of Jess was actually excited to see a pride in action like this.

Randy must have noticed that Jess's attention was no longer on him, and when he followed her line of sight and realized what was already in motion, he started screaming in a high-pitched voice that only stirred a disgust deep within her and made her subconscious rooting for the predators become a conscious one.

"There you are!" said a familiar voice behind her just as the lioness made her move. Jess gasped as she was jerked back from the platform, spun around, and pulled in to Mrs. Thomas's soft body. The woman held her close and secure, preventing her from seeing the goring that immediately followed below. But Jess could still hear the screams. They worked their way into her mind, creating a strange dissonance with the soft wool of Mrs. Thomas's sweater against her cheek. Even when the teacher pressed her hand firmly against Jess's ear to block out the sounds, Randy's screams muscled through.

You did that, didn't you?

YOU LEFT ME NO CHOICE.

I'm sorry.

DON'T BE. I'M NOT. HE DESERVED IT.

But he didn't do anything.

NOT THIS TIME. HE WOULD HAVE, THOUGH.

The screams stopped, and Jess knew that didn't bode

well for Randy. Mrs. Thomas loosened her grip on Jess but kept her from turning around. "Don't look. You don't need to see that."

"I didn't— I couldn't have stopped it."

"Hush. Are you okay?" Her firmly set jaw made Jess wonder if she was angry or if this was some new emotion Jess had never encountered before.

"Yeah, I'm fine."

Mrs. Thomas nodded, but her stern look didn't waver. "He didn't … he didn't *do* anything that you didn't like?"

"He touched my ears," Jess said, wondering if that qualified.

Mrs. Thomas opened her mouth to speak but closed it again and gazed over Jess's head toward the enclosure.

What would be left of Randy by the time rescuers arrived? The image of a carcass picked clean of everything but saggy gorilla teats flashed in Jessica's mind. She tamped it down, recognizing it as completely unrealistic; no self-respecting lion would leave that much fat on the bone.

Mrs. Thomas lifted Jess's chin to stare her in the eyes. "He deserved what he got, you understand me?"

Jess nodded and was now sure Mrs. Thomas wasn't angry with her, which was a relief. After one last look at the enclosure and a disgusted scowl, Mrs. Thomas shook her head slowly before leading Jess back down the stairs and away from lions' den.

Chapter Five

Jessica almost felt bad for not being more upset about what had happened at the zoo, but Destinee had the "upset" thing covered.

And now that they were in the car on the way home from Mooreson Elementary, Destinee's well of panic seemed to have dried up, and anger had taken its place. "It's a good thing those lions got him, or your mama would be locked up right now," she rambled from behind the steering wheel, glancing at her daughter and asking for the seventeenth time, "Are you sure he didn't touch you anywhere bad, Jess?"

"No, Mom," Jess replied impatiently. "Just the earlobes."

Destinee snarled. "Probably some fucked-up fetish. That son of a bitch ..."

LET HER KNOW I SAVED YOU.

Why?

JUST DO IT.

"God was the one who saved me. He pushed Randy over the edge."

Destinee's head snapped toward Jess. "Your father? He actually intervened?"

She nodded.

"Hm." Destinee's eyes flicked back to the road for just long enough to make sure the car was still in its lane. "And you know that for sure?"

"Yeah. He warned me not to go with Randy, but I didn't listen. And so he pushed Randy over the edge for touching my ears."

Destinee narrowed her eyes then nodded and faced the road again. "Hmm." She fidgeted in her seat. "Let him know I'd like to thank him personally before bed tonight."

Jess hadn't pegged her mom as a praying type, but she supposed it wasn't the strangest thing she'd heard. "I'm sure he already knows."

YES I DO. TELL HER I'LL SEE HER TONIGHT.

"He says he'll see you tonight."

Destinee bit her bottom lip but then jumped when her cell phone, which she always kept tucked between her thighs while she drove, began vibrating.

The car veered slightly as Destinee took her eyes off the road to check her phone and then swerved back into the lane as she sighed, accepted the call, and held it up to her ear.

"What is it now?"

Jess knew immediately who was on the other line. "What is it now?" was her mother's signature greeting whenever Jimmy Dean called. Jess had yet to actually meet

Jimmy in person—besides the one time she didn't remember, due to being a newborn—but she'd concocted a strong enough image of him in her mind based on the complaints Destinee regularly voiced against him. He was probably short and fat, and for some reason that she couldn't exactly pinpoint, she imagined he had one eye that never did look straight ahead. She also imagined he had holes in his clothes, but she knew where she'd come up with that detail. Jimmy was usually asking for something, money or otherwise, when he called Destinee. Other than those assumptions and the fact that Jimmy had been the chosen messenger from God, Jessica didn't know much about him. Someday, though, she hoped to meet him face-to-face, since he was the only other person she knew of who'd spoken directly with her dad.

Destinee gave Jimmy an earful over the phone. The man had gone and gotten himself into a financial hole again, that was obvious enough from the context. But this was nothing new, and Jess had enough to deal with, without worrying about Jimmy's verbal pummeling from her mother.

How was she even supposed to decide how she felt about the day's events when both her parents wouldn't shut up for a moment and let her think? At least with Destinee's attention temporarily focused on Jimmy, Jess only had one parent droning on …

God's lecture since she'd gotten back on the bus from the zoo, heading to Mooretown, had been so constant that it'd faded into a buzzing in the back of her mind as she tried to focus on other immediate tasks, like walking and responding to questions from the various adults who decided they needed to check in—school administrators and police officers and, over Mrs. Thomas's cell phone, a social worker and last but definitely not least (or calmest) her mother.

But now that the insanity and chaos had mostly subsided and Destinee's focus was diverted, Jess decided to tune back into God's lecture. She probably deserved it, anyway, after not listening to Him.

YOU KNOW HOW MANY PEOPLE WOULD KILL—AND HAVE KILLED, ACTUALLY—TO BE ABLE TO GAIN MY WISDOM AND ADVICE?

Is Luke going to be okay? She'd caught sight of him only once between when his uncle was mauled by lions and when she and the rest of her classmates, sans Luke, were loaded onto the bus to head back to Mooretown. The boy was sitting on a metal bench as Mrs. Thomas knelt in front of him, her hand resting gently on his arm as she crooned reassurance. The strangest part of it, and the one that left Jessica endlessly curious about what Mrs. Thomas was saying, was that Luke didn't look at all upset. In fact, he actually seemed to be holding back a smile.

God ignored her question. *AND YOU THINK YOU'RE TOO GOOD FOR IT. OUTRIGHT DISOBEYING ME. YOU KNOW WHAT HAPPENED TO THE FIRST ONE WHO OUTRIGHT DEFIED ME?*

No, what?

NO? HOW DO YOU NOT ... LUCIFER. LUCIFER DEFIED ME.

Who's that?

WHA— YOU DON'T KNOW WHO THAT IS?

Should I know?

ABSOLUTELY! IT'S ALL IN THE BIBLE!

But I haven't read the Bible. I didn't know I needed to. Should I?

ACTUALLY … NO. THERE WAS SOME STUFF SAID ABOUT WOMEN THAT— WELL, MAYBE WAIT FOR THE SECOND EDITION.

You mean you changed your mind about things?

HAVING A DAUGHTER CHANGES EVERYTHING. BUT THE POINT IS THAT NEXT TIME I SAY THOU SHALT NOT DO THINGS, YOU NEED TO LISTEN.

Does that mean I'm responsible for Randy's death?

NO, THAT'S ALL ME. AND I ENJOYED IT. THERE'S SOMETHING YOU SHOULD KNOW ABOUT RANDY.

Yeah?

HE WAS EVIL.

Evil? Like the Devil? While Jess didn't know much about religion, she knew her opposites, and since she knew about God, she also knew about the Devil.

YES, BUT HE WASN'T THE DEVIL.

That's good.

HE WAS A DEMON.

"Wait, *what?*"

Destinee paused between "fuh—" and "—king" to glance curiously at Jessica, who realized she'd spoken aloud. Jess waved her mom off, and Destinee was happy to oblige and get back to Jimmy. "Um, like I was saying, there's no fucking way we're doing that. Jess doesn't need church …"

What's the difference between a demon and the Devil?

FIRST AND FOREMOST, THE DEVIL ISN'T STUPID LIKE RANDY. BUT MOSTLY THERE ARE MANY DEMONS AND ONLY ONE DEVIL.

If Randy was a demon, she supposed she shouldn't worry about feeling bad for him. But before she could be completely alleviated of her guilt, she had to be sure.

Was Randy born a demon?

NO. BUT AT SOME POINT HE LET A DEMON INSIDE HIM.

Why would he do that?

HE DIDN'T MEAN TO.

Okay, so *there* was a new thing to be scared of. People could let demons inside them. She was pretty sure it couldn't happen to her, but other people around her could be in danger.

Are there a lot of people with demons in them?

OH YEAH. AND SOME OF THEM AREN'T POLITICIANS.

"I swear to God, Jimmy Dean"—Destinee's voice sliced through the conversation like a knife—"yes, God Himself. You know I'm thankful for you, but I don't owe you jack shit ... What?" Her eyes darted sideways to Jessica. "No. That was— that was a one-time thing. I thought we weren't gonna talk about that ever again."

More of the same.

Her mind returned to the important issues. *But how do I tell if someone's a demon?* She conjured up an image of Randy to see if there were signs she'd missed. Was it the donut around his middle? Did all demons have that? Probably not.

YOU'LL GET BETTER AT IT AS YOU GROW UP. THE GOOD NEWS IS THAT THERE ARE ALSO ANGELS. YOU HAVE A FEW IN YOUR LIFE ALREADY.

That's sorta creepy. Are there any around me right now? Jess searched the air vaguely.

NO.

What do angels look like?

THEY LOOK LIKE PEOPLE.

But with robes and wings and stuff, right?

NO WINGS, NO ROBES ... UNLESS THEY PUT ON A ROBE, I GUESS.

Her mental image of a man in a white robe with large, soft wings blinked out of her mind's eye instantly.

Oh. So like demons?

YES. THEY JUST LOOK LIKE REGULAR PEOPLE.

But they know they're angels?

EVENTUALLY THEY FIGURE IT OUT.

Did Randy know he was a demon?

NO. HEAVEN AND HELL WORK ON A DIFFERENT WAVELENGTH IN THE HUMAN BRAIN. THE MIND CAN SENSE GOOD AND EVIL. IT CAN BE INFLUENCED BY EITHER, BUT IT CAN BE WEEKS, MONTHS, OR EVEN YEARS BEFORE THE MIND KNOWS IT'S LOST CONTROL OF THINGS.

Knowing that, she actually felt a smidgeon of sympathy for Randy.

So does the Devil know he's the Devil?

OH HELL YEAH. THE DEVIL IS DIFFERENT.

I guess that's good ...

UH DUH. THAT'S WHY I MADE IT THAT WAY. THE

DEVIL WOULDN'T BE THE DEVIL IF HE DIDN'T COMMIT ALL HIS EVIL WITH A FULL UNDERSTANDING OF THE HARM IT CAUSED.

Cool.

SO WHILE WE'RE ON THE SUBJECT, THERE'S SOMETHING ELSE I NEED TO TELL YOU.

Jess sighed. *Please don't.*

YOU'LL NEED TO CONFRONT THE DEVIL EVENTUALLY.

Do I have to?

YES.

Damn it.

THAT'S THE SPIRIT.

What does the Devil look like? If the confrontation was inevitable, she should at least know what to expect. If the Devil had horns, he'd be easier to spot than demons.

WHATEVER YOU LEAST EXPECT HIM TO LOOK LIKE.

Crap.

THE DEVIL HAS TAKEN MANY FORMS IN THE PAST, BUT HE IS ALWAYS A WOLF IN SHEEP'S CLOTHING.

That sounds like just one form.

NO. IT'S A FIGURE OF SPEECH. I CAN SEE WHY YOU WOULD THINK THAT, THOUGH.

So the Devil isn't actually a wolf dressed in a sheep's shirt?

NOT EVEN A LITTLE BIT.

Then how will I recognize the Devil?

THAT'S THE WHOLE THING, ISN'T IT?

What whole thing?

WHY EVIL SUCKS.

He was being unhelpful again. Big shocker.

Destinee said, "Okay. You too, Jimmy," ended the call,

stared at the phone intensely for a moment, then slid it back between her thighs with a long exhale. "When I start going gray, Jess, it's because of that man."

"What did he want?"

Destinee shook her head vaguely. "Same thing as usual, money and for us to drive our asses out to Midland and go to church with him."

"You told him no."

"Hell yeah, I told him no. Don't worry, Jess, I wouldn't subject you to his Bible-thumping nonsense."

Something about that stung.

Being the only one who could hear God's voice all the time was exhausting and lonely. God always told her what to do, and now she knew that if she didn't listen, bad things could happen to those around her. She felt stuck. Isolated. No one else understood.

Except ...

God had led Jimmy Dean to Jessica's house the night she was born. Jimmy Dean had been given orders by God and had had to follow. And judging by his dedication to religion, there was a good possibility Jimmy Dean was *still* following orders from God.

She'd never considered it before, perhaps distracted by the usual avalanche of cursing that tumbled out of Destinee's mouth immediately following the words "Jimmy Dean," but maybe the man was the solution to two of Jessica's problems that seemed to be getting worse by the day: her isolation and her lack of knowledge about religion.

They were in the same boat.

She thought of the ark.

Hopefully not that kind of boat, filled with hungry diseased animals. But a good kind of boat. Maybe with healthy, well-fed animals. And David Attenborough to narrate.

She guessed Destinee wouldn't be okay with the existence of such a boat, so she proceeded cautiously. "I mean, I wouldn't mind meeting him sometime."

"Huh." Destinee seemed to consider the possibility.

"I mean, if it's fine with you. If not, that's okay too."

"If you wanna meet him, I guess that's all right." Destinee paused, shrugged. "He *was* in the room when you were born, while your daddy wasn't, so I guess that counts for something."

Jess returned her gaze back outside of the car.

Should I meet Jimmy Dean?

ABSOLUTELY.

Oh. Really? You think it's a good idea?

IF YOU USE THE TERM "GOOD" LOOSELY. VERY LOOSELY.

Huh? Why? Is Jimmy Dean the Devil?

THE LORD SHALL NOT SAY.

You can't tell me?

NO.

Is that because you don't know?

OF COURSE I KNOW.

Then why can't you tell me?

THAT'S NOT VERY GOOD SUSPENSE, IS IT?

Why does it have to be suspenseful?

BECAUSE THAT MAKES FOR A BETTER STORY. TRUST ME ON THIS. IF I'D TOLD YOUR HALF-BROTHER EVERY

SINGLE THING THAT WAS GOING TO HAPPEN, THE NEW TESTAMENT WOULDN'T HAVE SOLD A SINGLE COPY. NO ONE WOULD HAVE READ IT. EVERYONE WOULD STILL BE JEWS.

She thought of David from the park, the one who played safari so well. *Is being a Jew bad?*

OF COURSE NOT. THEY'RE MY CHOSEN PEOPLE.

She paused, letting the idea percolate. Chosen for what? And more importantly ...

But what about Christians?

THEY'RE MY CHOSEN PEOPLE TOO. I CHOOSE A LOT OF PEOPLE. LISTEN, YOU NEED TO FIND OUT THINGS FOR YOURSELF SOMETIMES SO THAT OTHER PEOPLE CAN LEARN LESSONS FROM IT.

That doesn't sound fair at all. What good is being your daughter if I still have to learn everything the hard way? At least give me a hint about the Devil.

FINE, BUT ONLY BECAUSE I WANT YOU TO WIN. AND BECAUSE I GET TO DO WHATEVER THE HEAVEN I WANT.

She didn't care what His reasons were, so long as she could get a little bit of help. *Okay. What's the hint?*

THE DEVIL'S NOT FROM MOORETOWN.

She thought about that, let it really sink in, before deciding that it was a fairly useless hint. She wasn't sure exactly how many people were on the face of Father's green earth, but she assumed it was a significantly larger number than were born in Mooretown. Possibly more than one million times larger.

What am I even supposed to do with that knowledge?

YOU CAN START BY CROSSING OFF ANYONE BORN IN MOORETOWN FROM YOUR DEVIL LIST.

Am I supposed to have one of those?

IT MIGHT BE A GOOD IDEA.

She reached down and grabbed her backpack from the floorboards, opening it and pulling out her school-issued daily planner before turning to November. Under that day's column was simply, *Zoo!!!!* Presently, she wrote down *finish homework* and *create devil list*.

Then she flipped to the notes section in the back of the planner and began writing the names of everyone she knew. Once she had twenty-five names, she jumped up to the top of the list and decided she might as well get started.

"Mom," she said, turning toward Destinee.

"Yeah, baby?"

"Where were you born?"

Destinee stared down at her strangely. "America."

"No, but where?"

"Here."

"Here as in Mooretown?" Jess asked anxiously.

"Yeah. Why?"

Jess beamed. "No reason. Just curious."

She waited until Destinee's focus was back on the road, then she crossed her mother's name off her Devil List.

Chapter Six

9 AGC

The knock on the front door was loud and abrupt, but not unexpected. Jess looked up from her fourth-grade math homework as Destinee stood from the couch where she and Jess had been waiting in the hour since lunch. Destinee paused and asked one last time, "You sure you're up for this? I can send his ass away, just give me the signal."

But Jess was secretly excited to finally talk with a man she'd heard about for the entirety of her life, though she knew better than to let that excitement show in front of her mom. So even though this meeting was months in the making, she said coolly, "No, it's fine. I don't mind."

Destinee searched her daughter's face and then nodded and crossed the living room to open the front door.

The man on the doorstep looked nothing like how Jess had imagined him, and for a moment she wondered if he was just a door-to-door salesman, not the actual guest.

"You're on time," Destinee said, surprised. "Come on in."

As Jimmy Dean took his first few steps inside the McCloud home, Jess got a better look at him. He defied all the expectations she'd built off the negative sentiments Destinee had expressed over the years. He was neither short nor fat and both his eyes moved in sync as he scanned the double-wide hesitantly. Rather than tattered rags, he wore a charcoal gray suit over a powder blue collared shirt, which brought out the blue of his eyes. He looked more like a businessman than a beggar, and Jess's mind tripped over itself trying to replace her previous image of him with this new one.

"Bet you never thought you'd be setting foot in this place again," Destinee said, clearly enjoying Jimmy's uneasiness.

"You're absolutely right," he said. His voice was like Aunt Jemima syrup poured over a bowl of Rice Krispies.

When his eyes landed on Jessica sitting at the end of the couch, her math homework still spread out on her lap, he inhaled sharply and took a step back like she'd snuck up on him.

"Jessica Christ ..." he breathed.

Wait. What did he just call her? Did he think that was her name?

Destinee motioned for Jess to come over, so she set her textbook and spiral notebook on the couch and approached slowly.

Jimmy looked almost as nervous as Jessica felt. She

hadn't expected to be sonervous. But she also hadn't expected Jimmy to be well groomed and tall.

He reached out and she shook his hand, forcing a smile.

"It's a pleasure to see you again, Jessica."

She wasn't sure how to respond. "You too."

Jimmy chuckled as he let go of her hand, and something about the way his eyes sparkled and the small parentheses that appeared around the corners of his mouth made it impossible for Jess to keep from smiling, too. She'd never met someone like Jimmy. She instinctively wanted to like him, but more than that, she wanted him to like her.

When his eyes landed on Destinee's bemused expression, the chuckling ceased immediately.

Jessica looked at her mom, whose arms were folded tightly across her chest as she uncharacteristically held her tongue. Why didn't her mother like Jimmy? He seemed so nice. Destinee had vocalized her many grievances against the man over the years, but Jessica could recall none of them. They probably weren't important. Sometimes her mother disliked people for reasons that seemed silly, so that was probably the case when it came to Jimmy.

He leaned over so he was on eye level, and she could smell his cologne, a strange combination of two scents that her brain registered as cedar and elevator. "How do you feel about ice cream?"

Jess's mind jumped back to the zoo, and she waited to see if God had anything to say. When she didn't hear from Him, she figured it was safe to proceed. "I love ice cream."

He straightened up again. "Dairy Queen then?" When

he glanced at Destinee, she shrugged one shoulder slightly and gave a nearly undetectable nod.

"Right-oh," he added. "Then, uh, I guess we should get to gettin'."

Destinee opened the door and Jimmy walked out first, but not before Destinee slipped him a folded-up bill (of which denomination, Jess couldn't see) and shot him one last stink eye as she mumbled, "Change comes back to me. I ain't playin'."

Jimmy grinned appeasingly and then headed out to his truck with Jess a step behind him.

Her nervousness began to gain momentum. What if Jimmy didn't like her? What if he wanted to like her but decided he couldn't?

Before Destinee shut the door, she hollered, "Jimmy."

He paused and turned around, his lips pressed together tightly, his jaw clenched.

"God's watching. Don't try anything."

Jimmy swallowed hard then forced a smile when his eyes traveled down to Jess. "Wouldn't dream of it," he said.

The Dairy Queen was on the other side of town, and as they sputtered along in Jimmy's old Tacoma, Jess began to feel like maybe this was another terrible decision. Maybe Jimmy *was* like Randy and God was just too busy with something else to stop her from going with him. She really wished she understood how all that worked with God being in more than one place at a time.

But Jimmy didn't seem like Randy, and not just because he had all his hair and wasn't soft and lumpy. Jimmy radiated energy all around him. Standing next to Randy had felt nothing like that; it was like he was sucking energy from his surroundings. It reminded her of the big coin donation funnel at the pharmacy where Destinee worked— you dropped a coin into a slot and it rolled around in smaller and smaller spirals down the sloping plane, moving toward the small hole in the center, circling frantically in a tight death throe before plummeting through the hole and into the coin basket at the bottom.

Jimmy and Randy couldn't be the same thing. And because Randy was a demon, she deduced that Jimmy could not also be a demon.

So maybe it was just the fact that she didn't have the slightest idea what to talk about with him that left her anxious.

"So Jess," he said, breaking the ice as they turned right at the stoplight at the edge of her neighborhood, "I'm curious what your mother's told you about me."

"Um. Nothing much. Just that God sent you to tell her I was his child."

Jimmy nodded. "Yep. Messenger from God. Guilty!" He chuckled and lifted his hands briefly from the steering wheel in a don't-shoot motion. "What else?"

Jess knew better than to mention the way Destinee had griped about him over the years. "That's it."

"All right, all right ... She'd just mentioned that you wanted to meet me, so I was wondering why that might be."

"I wanted to meet someone else who'd met my dad."

Jimmy nodded gravely. "Daddy issues. May they unite us all."

"I don't have daddy issues," she protested. She wasn't sure what exactly daddy issues were, but the way Jimmy said it made it sound like something bad.

He sighed. "No, trust me, Jessica. You have daddy issues, whether you realize it or not."

"Did you see him?"

"Huh?"

"God. When he talked to you, did you see him or just hear him?"

"Oh, I saw Him. Hard to miss Him, actually." Jimmy chuckled to himself, but she wasn't sure why that was funny.

"What did he look like?"

Jimmy's head remained forward facing while his eyes rolled sideways in his skull to glance down at her. There was a moment's hesitation. "Uh ... well, He was ... He had brown hair."

It was almost nothing, but it was more than she'd ever gotten about the way God looked, and she chomped at it like a starving gator would a slice of white bread. "Like mine?"

"Umm, a little darker. And coarser."

They turned into the Dairy Queen parking lot.

"And what about his eyes?"

Jimmy squinted and pouted his lips while he accessed his memory. "Brown, I think."

"Like mine!" She actually looked like God! She hadn't expected it to be such a big relief.

But that was all he said before he shut off the engine and opened the driver's door.

Jess climbed out of the truck. She wanted to keep shooting off questions, but she knew adults got sick of that quickly, and she didn't want Jimmy to get sick of her, so she occupied herself with imagining God as a tall brown-eyed brunet.

At least once they were inside, the urge to pester Jimmy with a thousand questions was tempered by the need to inspect the menu. In the end, Jess settled on a vanilla Blizzard with M&Ms and Jimmy ordered a chocolate dipped cone and they waited in silence for the order to be filled before Jess led the way over to a booth not far from the front door.

As she began skimming off the top of her Blizzard, Jimmy hesitantly began conversation with, "So, you get good grades in school?"

What a silly question. But then she remembered he was an adult, and that's the kind of question adults liked to ask. "Yes."

"What's your favorite subject?"

"Math," she said without pause, glancing up from her ice cream to see if he approved.

"Math? Really? Seems like you might be more into … I dunno, art or something."

What the heck was that supposed to mean? "No, I like math. I'm good at it, too."

Something seemed to click for Jimmy, and the eyebrow he'd hitched up at her initial response relaxed back into place. He nodded. "Ah, I see. God help you with that?"

She tried to glare at him the way she'd seen Destinee do to men who were rude to her at her job at the pharmacy, but Jess wasn't sure if she'd pulled it off. "No. I can do math myself. It's not hard."

Jimmy exhaled and leaned back in his seat. He dragged his fingers through his perfectly slicked-back hair without compromising the shape of it. "All right ... all right. I never was very good at math. Or anything. I wasn't the greatest student when I was your age. Hardly went to school. Guess that might've been a factor."

Jessica hadn't considered that, at some point in time, Jimmy had been a kid just like her. The mention of him being her age exposed her to a new set of questions she wanted to rapid-fire at him all at once. Maybe she could even learn something about him that helped her understand why God had chosen him as His messenger. She had so many riddles in her life, it might be nice to put one to rest.

She remembered her Devil List, which she'd become rather lax on after it'd repeatedly proved useless in helping her identify the Devil, and she asked, "Where are you from?"

Jimmy bit into his dipped cone, sending cracks through the hard chocolate shell so that he had to tilt his head and the cone to keep the chocolate from falling onto the table.

He stuck all the coating in place and wiped his mouth with a napkin. "Mobile, Alabama, or just south of it. Grew up in a little town where ..." His voice trailed off after Jess heard the bell above the front door jingle behind her. His eyes jolted open when they landed on whoever had just walked in. "Well, fuck," he mumbled.

Did Jimmy know people in Mooretown outside of Jess

and her mother? She turned to see what had caused Jimmy to stop mid-sentence, and when she spotted the Wursts, all four of them, she instantly shared his sentiment. But wait. How did he know the Wursts?

Courtney buried her head in a BlackBerry, a satisfied grin on her face as she typed furiously. Jess wondered who she was cyberbullying. Meanwhile, Trent bounced around, tugging on Mrs. Wurst's shirt and prattling off some nonsense order he wanted that included a burger, fries, a coke, and something about peanut butter ice cream with cookie dough, bananas, and caramel. He *would* order something that mismatched and vomit-worthy.

It was eventually Trent, his gaze constantly darting around like a pyro searching for a gas stove, who was the first to spot Jess. She tried to turn away before he could recognize her, but she failed.

"Hey, it's—" he yelled, before pausing. Maybe he'd forgotten her name or how much he enjoyed antagonizing her.

But instead of *her* name being the next word off his lips, he finished with, "Reverend Dean?"

Reverend Dean? Could Trent be mistaking Jimmy with someone else? Maybe a brother who looked like him? She knew Jimmy went to church, but even with her minimal understanding of what a reverend actually was, Jimmy didn't fit the bill. Not one bit.

Jess kept her back to the Wursts, but she could feel their approach. Her eyes darted up to Jimmy, who shifted in his seat, sitting up straighter now, carefully setting his dipped cone on the table before wiping the chocolate from his hands onto his napkin. Something had changed about him, and not just his posture. His face softened but his jaw strengthened, and he looked confidently toward the Wursts as a small, gentle smile landed gracefully on his lips.

"Reverend," said the man next to Trent.

She'd only ever seen Mr. Wurst that one *unfortunate* time—and never in person. He looked much more dignified with clothes on, though, especially a police uniform like the one he was wearing as he stood next to the table, towering over her as she continued to silently spoon ice cream into her mouth.

Jimmy stood from the booth and extended his hand. "Chief Wurst. What a surprise." The panic that had slipped onto Jimmy's face moments before was nowhere to be seen now. He nodded at Mrs. Wurst. "Ruth. Good to see you again."

"It's been since last Sunday since I've seen you," she blurted stiffly.

A thin cord of a muscle flexed in Jimmy's neck. "Indeed." Was he as confused by her greeting as Jess was? Jimmy turned his attention back to the police chief. "I didn't realize you lived in Mooretown," he said conversationally.

Mr. Wurst stood closest to the table, his wife a few steps behind with a hand on each of her children's shoulders. Jessica suspected Ruth's grip had more to do with holding them still than any affection for the two monsters.

Courtney's attention was no longer on her phone, and she looked like she smelled a rotten egg as she crinkled her nose and glared at Jessica. Trent appeared dangerously confused as his attention jumped back and forth between the two occupants at the table.

Chief Wurst said, "Sure am, Reverend. Born and raised here."

"And you make the drive to Midland every weekend?"

He nodded confidently. "I'll admit, when Ruth first saw you on the news, read about you on the Internet, and said we need to attend, I was skeptical. But now I'd drive to Carlsbad each week if it meant hearing your sermons."

Jimmy swallowed hard. "Carlsbad? Why Carlsbad?" The curt words broke rhythm with the easy conversation, erupting quickly and curtly.

Mr. Wurst seemed to notice the deviation, too, and he frowned and shook his head, blinking quickly. "Just ... it was just an example."

"Ah yes, an example." Jimmy's grin returned. "Never been to Carlsbad myself. Never had any interest. None at all."

"What're you doing with Jessica?" Trent finally blurted. Mrs. Wurst's fingers dug into her son's shoulder and he flinched and moaned softly.

"Oh, psh." Jimmy waved off Trent playfully. "Come now ... little boy,"—Jimmy's inability to remember Trent's name provided a welcome dose, albeit a small one, of satisfaction for Jess—"if you'd been paying attention to my sermons, you would already know."

The rest of the Wursts nodded knowingly, but considering they'd just been waiting with equally eager expressions for Jimmy's response, Jess decided they were full of it and felt another jolt of satisfaction at seeing Trent's entire family hang him out to dry.

Trent remained speechless and then Jimmy said words that made zero sense to Jess. *"Sumus omnes porcos, sed Deus est Aper."*

Chief Wurst chuckled deep in his chest and rustled Trent's silky blond hair like he'd been expecting Jimmy to say that.

Who in her Father's name would've expected Jimmy to say that nonsense? Those weren't words. At least not English words. What the heck?

But Trent acted like he understood, ahh-ing and nodding slowly before chuckling cruelly like he was actually in on the joke. Courtney smirked at Jess, and Mrs. Wurst's nostrils flared as she inhaled deeply and shifted where she stood, her eyes like laser beams as they swept over Jimmy from head to foot to head again.

"Well, we won't keep you two, then," Chief Wurst said. "See you tomorrow, Reverend."

"Yes. Look forward to it." Jimmy nodded one last time to the Mooretown Police Chief, who then herded his family away from the table.

Once Jimmy settled himself back into the booth, Jess rounded on him. "You're a reverend?"

Jimmy nodded proudly. "Sure am. Reverend Jimmy Dean. If only my mom could see me now ... that hag."

"What were those words you said just a second ago?"

"Huh?" He picked up his cone, which now had snow-white cream melting out from under the chocolate and dripping down the sides. He licked it up and slurped out the rest of the liquid before starting on the chocolate exterior again.

"That thing you said. What did it mean?"

He waved her off. "Aw, nothing. Just a Bible thing. You probably already know it."

"How would I already know it?"

"Well, it's probably something God's already taught you. I, uh, well, your mother said you can talk to Him."

Jess nodded. "Sure, but he doesn't really teach me things."

Jimmy reclined and threw an arm over the back of the booth. "So you don't know about the Bible? You don't know about God's Word?"

She shrugged. "I mean, I know some of his words. Sometimes I feel like he never shuts up."

Jimmy chuckled and nodded. "Yeah, that makes sense." Then a thought seemed to occur to him, and he leaned forward, his brows furrowing slightly. "Hey, what would you say about coming to church with me sometime?"

Jess froze with the spoon in her mouth. Church? Why would she go to church? She dipped the spoon back into the cup and cocked her head slightly to the side. "I don't know …"

He smacked the table excitedly. "Oh come on! It would be fun! Your mom is welcome to come with you. Y'all would be my guests of honor!"

While there were big possibilities around that idea—Jess being the guest of honor at a church the Wursts apparently attended—something about it still didn't feel right.

He held up his left palm, reassuringly. "No need to give a yes or no right away. Just think about it. You are always welcome in my church." He sighed. "You know, I understand you're God's daughter, but since I was there for your birth, I've always sort of thought of you as my daughter, too. I mean, as much as I can, considering this is the first time I've seen you since you were a fresh little slimeball."

"Huh?"

"When you were born. You were … wait, how old are you?"

"Nine."

"Ah, right. Okay. So you probably don't know about babies and all that yet. Well, never mind. The point is that I feel protective of you, like a father would. And I just want what's best for you, so if you decide to come visit White Light Church, there'll always be a place for you in the pews."

Jess felt warmth radiating from his smile that seemed to penetrate her chest. Okay, so she couldn't cross off his name from her mental Devil List, but surely the daughter of God couldn't feel this sort of glowing affection for the Devil himself. And he thought of her as his daughter. Could she think of him as a father? Sure, she technically already had a father, but she never saw Him in the flesh. Maybe Jimmy really *could* be like a dad to her, because at least he was here, walking and talking.

Right on cue, *He* showed up.

JIMMY IS NO FATHER TO YOU.

Have you ever taken me to ice cream?

NO, BUT AT LEAST I DON'T CONSTANTLY ASK YOUR MOTHER FOR MONEY LIKE HE DOES.

You don't exactly chip in, either.

TRUST ME, JIMMY IS NO ONE TO GROW ATTACHED TO.

You're just jealous that I like him better.

"Jess?"

"Huh?"

Jimmy was looking at her strangely. She'd spaced out again.

"Did you ... wait. Were you ... are you talking to Him?"

Not wanting to divulge her thoughts, she shook her head. "No, just thinking about school."

"Ah. Okay." But he didn't seem convinced as he flicked the last bit of his cone into his mouth and crunched down. "Well, I really do need to get back to Midland and finish my sermon for tomorrow. Shall we?"

Jess scooped the rest of her ice cream into her mouth and nodded enthusiastically, then the two of them slid out of the booth, tossed their trash, and headed out toward the truck, but not before Jimmy threw a quick wave to the Wursts, who waved back enthusiastically from the booth at the opposite side of the restaurant.

As Jimmy drove Jess home, he regaled her with stories from his early years on the road. She listened quietly as he conjured scenes she could practically smell and taste. When he described his year in the Ozark Mountains, going door-to-door for the IRS (whatever that was), she could hear the crisp air as it sifted through the dense foliage and created soft ripples across the surface of a spring-fed stream. And when he described the day he'd walked off a construction site in the Bayou after a gator snuck up and nearly chomped his left foot, Jessica could see the individual speckles around the alligator's nose, smell the earthy must of the swamp, feel sweat-soaked clothes clinging to her body.

"Then where did you go?" she asked.

"Ehh … West. A story for another time." He grinned confidently at her as they pulled into the McCloud driveway. "Well, it was a pleasure. Sorry it took this long for us to catch up."

"It's okay," Jess said brightly.

"If you want, we can do this more often." He eyed her cautiously, then quickly added, "But only if you want. It's totally up to you."

"Yeah, that sounds fun."

He laughed. "And who can say no to ice cream, really?"

Jess flashed him one last smile then hopped out of the truck. When she walked inside, Destinee was still in the same place on the couch.

She muted the TV as she turned toward her daughter. "Hey, baby, how was it?"

"Fun!" Jess said. "I got a Blizzard and Jimmy got a dipped cone, and then we saw—"

"Did he give you the change?" she interrupted.

"What?"

"God dammit. I gave that bastard a twenty. Of course he got himself the cheapest damn thing and kept the change." Destinee sighed. "Sorry, what were you about to say?"

But Jess didn't feel like talking about it anymore. "Nothing. It was fun, is all."

"And he didn't … he didn't say anything that you didn't like or ask you any questions you didn't want to answer?"

What was with the suspicion? Jess felt heat rush into her face. "No. He was nice. Why didn't you tell me he was a reverend?"

Destinee pursed her lips then sighed. "Because he's not a real reverend, baby. He's just a fake one."

"Why do you hate Jimmy so much?" she snapped, as an inarticulate rage knotted her stomach.

Destinee recoiled, leaning back and crossing one leg over the other. "I don't hate him. I just … I'm not his biggest fan is all."

"I like him," Jess proclaimed before turning on her heels and stomping off to her room.

But once she got inside and had crawled under her covers, her head began to swim. She hadn't meant to be mean to her mom. But life could be so much easier if Destinee and Jimmy got along. Maybe they could fall in love, too. Would God be okay with that?

He can have a say in it when he takes me out to ice cream.

She sat up in bed again, flipped on the TV to Animal Planet and let a British man's soothing voice croon on about lemurs until she nodded off.

Chapter Seven

11 AGC

"Get your ass up, Jess! You knew this was coming. Not my fault you stayed up late watching TV."

Jess cracked one eye open before Destinee flicked on the lights and blinded her. "Mom! Stop! Ugh." She pulled the blanket over her head.

"Listen, baby, this was your idea."

"I changed my mind. I don't want to go anymore." Anxiety had kept Jess awake until nearly three in the morning, and now her body was so tired it felt like her organs weighed a hundred pounds each.

"Too late. We're committed. If we don't show, that grifter of a clergyman won't give me no peace about it. And I swear to God that if I get one more voicemail from Jimmy, I'm just gonna have to kill him. We either gotta go, or I gotta kill him. One of those will land you living with Grandma."

"Ugh." The prospect of living with crabby Granny McCloud out in her El Paso trailer park was enough to get Jess out of bed any day. Because while she doubted that Destinee would actually kill Jimmy Dean, she didn't doubt it *completely*.

"Hurry now. We leave in thirty minutes. Don't spend all of it on your hair."

Having made herself clear, Destinee shut the bedroom door behind her and Jess slowly pulled herself from her bed. There'd been a documentary on Bengal tigers that had started after Jess should have already been asleep and lasted much longer than a normal person would want a Bengal tiger documentary to last. But not Jess. Tigers were no giraffes, but they were still interesting enough to keep her mind off her anxious thoughts and give her racing heart a break. Why was she so nervous about seeing Jimmy's church? They'd gone out to ice cream together a handful of times since he'd first started coming around two years before, and she'd begun to feel comfortable with him, even daring to indulge him with a little inside information from God Himself. Nothing too important. Just answers to a few of Jimmy's random questions, like whether it was okay to eat pigs now, why it still wasn't okay to eat pigs, why pigs are so dirty when they're actually more intelligent than dogs, whether pigs feel pain, etc. So mostly just pig stuff.

The first time pigs entered into the conversation, God had gladly provided the information, but each time they came up after that, God ranted about smiting and "grand" plans that kept Him from smiting. So Jess was forced to pretend He wasn't around. Eventually, He stopped coming around, and Jess was left to study pigs on the Internet before each ice cream date with Jimmy so that she could answer his questions herself. She'd become quite the swine expert.

She'd also learned a little about Jimmy's past. He'd grown up on a farm then hopped a train and hit the road when he was only twelve because his mother married his pastor, which was, for some unnamed reason, not okay with Jimmy.

But that was all Ice Cream Jimmy. Having glimpsed Reverend Dean when the Wursts had shown up on their first outing, Jess already knew that Church Jimmy wasn't the same as Ice Cream Jimmy.

But Ice Cream Jimmy was persuasive, and it was that man who'd convinced Jess to convince her mother that they should go visit Church Jimmy.

Jessica groaned and stared helplessly at her closet, wondering what on earth one was expected to wear to a church, let alone one who happened to be the daughter of the deity everyone was there to worship.

Probably something nice. That narrowed it down quite a bit, considering she only owned two dresses and one had stopped fitting her properly about six months before.

The red cotton dress it was. Thankfully, it had been a warm February so far, because the sleeveless dress wouldn't have worked otherwise, and she'd be faced with a problem much too tricky for how tired she was.

They were ten minutes late getting out the door. Destinee wasn't happy about it, but she could easily make it up on the drive from Mooretown to Midland. Jess stared out the window and called to God to come talk, but he wasn't anywhere to be found. Typical. She'd watched shows late at night (always after Destinee was already asleep and Animal Planet was showing some dumb thing on bugs or humans) where terrible things would happen and people would ask questions like, "Where is God now?" or "How could God let this happen?" Jess knew the feeling all too well. She was the daughter of God, for His sake, and in times like these, when she was at her most desperate, He was almost never anywhere to be found. She wanted to pin Him down on it, really interrogate Him, but every time she grilled Him on topics like that, He would say, *OH HEY, I NEED TO GO DEAL WITH A TSUNAMI,* or something along those lines, *and then there would actually be one.* Jess was never certain if she had terrible timing or if God actually created disasters as an excuse to get out from under her thumb, but the whole set of coincidences left her hesitant to ask Him tough questions.

Her mom, though, couldn't use natural disasters as a diversion tactic, so it was often during times like these, when they were both stuck in the close proximity of the car, that Jess chose to strike.

Without removing her eyes from the road ahead of them, Jess asked, "Mom, why haven't we ever been to church?"

Destinee glanced over dubiously. "Why *would* we go? You're the daughter of God. I guess I just figured you're kind of, I dunno, church wherever you go."

"But some of the kids at school say that you have to go to church to get into Heaven."

"Those kids are full of shit and need to dislodge the stick from their asshole. Which kids are saying that?"

Jess knew better than to name names. "Just a few. Doesn't matter."

"Why don't you ask *your father* about it?" she replied sardonically.

Jess shrugged. "He doesn't like it when I ask tough questions."

Destinee scoffed. "Figures. He seems allergic to committing to anything. I should have guessed that the night we met."

"Wait, you *met* God?" Maybe it was because she had never seen the two of them talk, but Jess always assumed that God had never physically introduced Himself to her mother. She'd assumed Jimmy was the only other person she knew who'd met God in the flesh and could talk about it with her. How had she not known this until now?

Destinee's brow furrowed and she looked at Jess. "Of course we met. He ... got me pregnant. Do you know how people get pregnant, Jess?"

Jess in fact did not. She knew how a lot of other animals got pregnant, but it didn't seem dignified enough for humans. "Is it the same way that giraffes do it?"

"Um ... yeah, that's one position. Anyway. It doesn't matter. All I'm saying is that your father has a problem with commitment. That's all I'm saying. Let's not talk about it anymore."

So Jess was left to imagine how humans would make a baby like giraffes do, which wasn't her favorite mental exercise but was intriguing nonetheless, until she caught her first glimpse of the dazzling metropolis that was Midland, Texas.

Had Dallas been this large and had so many giant, reflective structures? She couldn't remember. She had likely been too caught up in her zoo to-see list to even look up at the sights outside the school bus windows, and, for obvious reasons, she hadn't been paying much attention to anything outside of her head on her way home from that field trip years ago.

But she suspected not even Dallas was as bustling as Midland on a Sunday morning. How many people lived here?! It must be at least ten thousand!

Massive shiny buildings spread across the horizon as they approached downtown. What could possibly necessitate so many big buildings all in one place? She'd seen big cities like Los Angeles and Chicago in pictures and movies, but it was a whole different animal to see a place like this in person. What would it be like to live somewhere with this many people? Would she even know all their names? She guessed not. And on the flip side of that, not everyone would know *her* name. Hope welled up inside her at the prospect of someday living where she could go unnoticed.

Traffic was at a standstill on the frontage road leading up to White Light Church. The parking lot was the biggest Jess had ever seen, just like most things in Midland. Were all these people really here just to listen to Jimmy speak? She supposed *she* liked Jimmy pretty well, but she'd never heard him say anything that would draw this big of a crowd. Maybe other important things happened in church, too.

The anxiety had formed a tight knot in her chest by the time she closed the car door behind her and started the long trek from the back of the parking lot to the front doors of the church.

"Oh Jesus fucking Christ," Destinee said as they approached the front of the building. "You gotta be fucking kidding me."

A well-dressed family of four walking a few paces ahead gasped and looked back over their shoulders, and Jess wondered what their problem was. Destinee didn't even seem to notice, though, and when Jess followed her mother's gaze, she understood immediately what had caused the exclamation.

The statue. It sat atop a massive stone archway that people had to walk underneath to enter the church. The morning sun acted like stage lighting, making each detail pop and casting a long dark shadow behind it that pointed to the glass front doors of White Light. Jess couldn't pull her eyes from the figure. It was a tall, thin man—perhaps just larger than life-size—his arms outstretched in either direction to form a T with his body. "Is that Jesus?" She wondered aloud. She'd seen her fair share of depictions of her half-brother, and this one didn't much resemble those in the face. But then she realized who it actually was.

Destinee muttered, "God dammit, Jimmy."

"Why would he make a statue of himself?"

"More like, how's he gonna hit me up for money for

years, never pay me back, and *then* make a statue of himself?"

Jess didn't have an answer for that.

Once they were only a few yards away from the arch, Jess noticed words carved into it. She and her mother paused to stare, forcing the sea of traffic to part around them as it flowed by. Carved at the very top of the arch was *White Light Church* and underneath that, *Sumus omnes porcos, sed Deus est Aper.* She tried to sound it out but quickly realized there was no point. It wasn't English.

But then she recognized one of the words. *Porcos.* Where'd she seen that before? Of course! In her swine research for Jimmy. It still didn't make much sense, though. Who would build a monument to himself and then carve something about pigs into it?

Jimmy, I guess.

She was starting to seriously question if she understood what church was actually about.

After reading the inscription once more, she asked Destinee what it meant.

Destinee squinted and moved her lips as she tried to read it. "Hell if I know. I dropped out in high school, and I sure as shit never took Spanish."

So they gave up guessing and passed on under the arch, and as they did so, Jess's skin started to tingle. At first, she thought she'd managed to walk into a cloud of gnats, but after a few swipes at her arms to no avail and noticing that no one else was swiping at their arms, she realized it might be something else causing the sensation. And as they entered through one of the multiple sets of glass double doors leading inside, the tingling intensified, and her skin felt like it was buzzing. It made her nose itch and her eyes water.

Or maybe it was how bright everything was that made her eyes water. Inside the foyer she found herself surrounded by glass and white and more glass and sunlight and more white. Jess had never been anywhere like this. It felt like the world was disappearing around her, like God had come in with a big eraser and got to work on everything except the people.

"This is like walking into a damn hospital," Destinee whispered to Jess. "What do you reckon their Windex budget is in a place like this?"

Even the people were all white—not their clothes, but everything else about them. Those in the foyer greeting each member had teeth as shiny and reflective as the walls and seemed to enjoy showing off said teeth in a gesture that Jess knew was intended to show warmth and acceptance but still conjured an image of a timber wolf defending its territory from another alpha.

A young man and woman approached them, teeth-first. "Welcome! I don't recognize you two, are you new?" asked the woman, whose blonde hair was slicked back perfectly flat into a tight ponytail.

"Yeah," Destinee said curtly.

"Oh, well, that's no big deal," the man said. He didn't seem like any man Jessica had met. He used his hands a little too much when he was talking—maybe that was it. Or maybe it was how wide he opened his mouth to form each new sound. Or maybe it was the wild look in his eyes that made Jess wonder if he was actually seeing her when he was looking straight at her, and if she was actually seeing him when she stared back into his brown eyes. "We see newcomers all the time, don't we, Diane?" He laughed, his big, white teeth reflecting sunlight every which way. Jess had no clue what he was laughing about.

"We sure do! I'm Diane, and this is Bradley. What're your names?"

Jess's skin buzzed too much for her to feel like chatting, but luckily she didn't have to.

"Destinee. And this is my daughter Jessica."

"Destinee?!" yelled Bradley with a big, stupid grin. "What a wonderful name! Well, it sounds like it was your *destiny* to end up at White Light, and we're glad to have you! How did you hear about us?"

Jess kept her gaze glued to her mom so she didn't have to look at Bradley's big, dumb face anymore. It was clear that Destinee was waging a war against rolling her eyes. Jess was surprised she hadn't yet. "We know Jimmy—I mean, Reverend Dean."

"Ohhh," said Diane, looking at Bradley.

"Ohhh," said Bradley, looking back at Diane. "Well," he continued, "that's certainly ... you actually *know* him?"

"Yeah, we go back a little ways," Destinee said, sounding unsure.

"Wait." Revelation swept over Bradley's face. "Are you *the* Destinee?"

"We got to go." Destinee grabbed Jess's hand and pulled her forward into the thick crowd that was hurrying into the chapel. "Batshit crazy, all of them," she mumbled.

Traffic bottlenecked through the doors leading into the sanctuary, but once they were through, Jess was finally able to take in the sheer size of the place.

Destinee pulled her to the side and out of the traffic while they assessed where to sit. That allowed Jessica a moment to work out some quick multiplication. She counted heads in one of the packed pews. Twelve. She counted the number of pews per row. Twenty. She counted the number of rows. Four. Twelve times twenty was obviously two hundred and forty. Then times four.

Nine hundred and sixty people could fit in the pews.

Why in her father's name would nine hundred and sixty people want to listen to anything Jimmy had to say?

Before she was able to answer her own question, her mother's voice interrupted her thoughts. "Oh Christ." Destinee stared straight ahead at the altar.

"What?" Jess couldn't see over the heads of the group in front of them. "What is it?"

"Nothing." Destinee dragged her back into the flow of people before quickly pulling her into one of the pews farthest from the stage. "Let's just grab a seat and get this over with."

But before they could scoot more than a foot away from the aisle, a familiar voice boomed over the crowd, stopping Destinee in her tracks. "Could it be?" It had the omnipresence of God's voice, but based upon her mother's reaction to it, Jess was pretty sure it wasn't in her mind. Destinee's shoulders slumped, and that's when it clicked: the voice was coming through giant white speakers hung around the ceiling.

"Are my eyes deceiving me?" the voice said again, except this time she heard the man himself more clearly than the speakers.

Destinee turned toward the voice. "No, Jimmy, they're not."

Reverend Dean didn't have to snake through the crowds like Destinee and Jess had; instead, the crowds parted for him so that he was able to easily glide over to where they stood at the edge of the pews.

He looked much less like a salesman now, having exchanged his usual charcoal-gray suit for one that was as white as everything else in the church. Even the headset he wore hooked over his dome, curving down to hover an inch from his mouth so that not a single crucial word of his went unheard by all, was entirely white. The only exception to his uniform attire was the red cord draped around his neck that hung down his front and had a cloven hoof dangling from each end.

Onlookers watched in awe as Jimmy directly addressed the newcomers. "I am so excited that you were able to make it today for this joyous anniversary." He placed his hands on Destinee's shoulders and smiled kindly at her. "You are an honored guest." Then he turned to Jessica, who wished she had dressed all in white so that she could blend in with the walls and pews and floor and perhaps escape notice completely. "Child." He bit his lip and his nostrils flared like he might cry. She really, *really* hoped he did not. "Words cannot describe what seeing you here, on this momentous occasion, stirs within me. You are a beautiful child of God."

While Jess's brain scrambled to reconcile Ice Cream Jimmy with whoever the heck this guy was, Destinee's resolve gave out and she rolled her eyes. "Well, she *is* THE child of God, so—"

"Ha!" Jimmy patted Destinee's shoulder. "Good one. If you'll excuse me, I need to start the service." He breezed past them, and the sea of parishioners parted to allow him easy passage up to the stage.

As he approached it, the crowd took the hint and quickly filed into the pews. It wasn't until those in the rows ahead of her sat down that Jess was finally able to get a good glimpse of the altar.

Two long windows let light stream in from outside, reflecting off of all the white surfaces on the stage where Jimmy took his place. It seemed like an awfully big stage for one man.

There was one object in particular that stood out against the blank palette, though, and Jess had to squint to be sure it was what she thought it was. But no, sure enough, it was exactly what she thought it was.

On the wall between the two windows, just visible above where Jimmy Dean stood on the pulpit, was a giant, mounted hog's head.

And now Jimmy's pig questions started to gain context, though they were still far from making any real sense in her mind.

She tugged on Destinee's dress. "Why's that up there?"

Destinee grabbed Jess and made her sit, since most everyone else was by now. "I couldn't tell you," she whispered, "but I'd bet we'll find out."

Jimmy adjusted his headset minutely before beginning. "Welcome." He outstretched his arms to his congregation and let the word resonate through the large space until a small echo repeated his welcome from the opposite side of the room.

"I am so pleased that each and every one of you could make it on this very special day. As some of you may be aware, today is White Light Church's tenth anniversary!" He motioned with a wafting of his hands for the audience to cheer, and cheer they did.

Although she'd never been to church, she'd naturally assumed there would be less cheering in it. She let her eyes wash over the heads of the congregation until she spotted four familiar heads just a few rows forward and to the left. The Wursts.

It wasn't as if she hadn't expected to see them here, but that didn't make her any happier about it. A small part of her had held out hope that this would be the Sunday they all got the stomach flu and had to stay home.

"Yes, ten years ago, we held our first service to worship *the* Deus Aper, as some like to think of Him—myself included." He chuckled and smiled, and the audience returned the favor.

"Why are they laughing?" Jess whispered to her mother.

One of Destinee's eyebrows was hitched up slightly, and she almost looked amused. "It's called kissing ass."

Jimmy's posture softened as he clasped his hands humbly in front of him and walked over to the stairs leading down from the tall stage. "It was eleven and a half years ago that God came to me." He took a seat on the top stair and gazed out over the crowd. "He said that there was something important for me to do for Him."

None of this was news to Jess, so it still didn't fill in the blanks on why Jimmy had started White Light Church.

"Many of you know the basics, but today, I'm going to tell you the whole story, the Hog's honest truth." He let that sink in, and if there was a noise level quieter than silence, the congregation had achieved it. "You see, I was a sinner. A dirty, *filthy* sinner. I was fleeing those sins when God came to me on the open road. I was desperate, my car had crashed into a ditch, I had no money, no friends. And when I say *Deus Aper*, when I say that we are all pigs, but God is Hog, I mean it." His honey-smooth voice cracked before he placed a hand over his heart and bit his lip. "He created us in His image, sure. But look what we've amounted to. So when God spoke to me"—he stood up and stared the fourth wall right in the eyes—"He chose the most deplorable animal in this state—the scourge on our environment that does nothing but eat, mate, and fight—as the vessel for His Word. Why? Because He knew that's what I'd become—what we've *all* become! And in His infinite mercy and grace, He was willing to *degrade* Himself to this lowly form to ensure that we heard and understood His message." His voice had risen, and Jess felt like she was being scolded, but she didn't know what she'd done.

"And I heard Him, all right. Blood of the Hog, how I heard Him!" His voice shook. Was he about to cry? Why was he about to cry? None of this made much sense. "We *are* a bunch of pigs. He didn't tell me this—no. He *showed* me this. In His infinite wisdom, He navigated me to the home of Destiny herself. And when I say Destiny, I mean exactly what you think. Inside that house I could hear blasphemy spewing from the mouth of a sow birthing her piglet."

"What the fuck?" Destinee whispered sharply.

"And when I knocked on the door, you know what greeted me?" He paused for dramatic effect, allowing each member to imagine what swine-related horror could have possibly loomed.

"A shotgun barrel to the chest." He mimed lowering a shotgun at the audience, lining up the sights, finger on the trigger. Then he lowered the imaginary gun, frowned, and shook his head. "This was how the messenger of God was greeted by one of His creations. This is what we've come to."

WHAT'D I MISS?

I'm not honestly sure. Wait, why are you asking me? You're God.

OF COURSE I AM. IT'S CALLED MANNERS. NO ONE LIKES A KNOW-IT-ALL.

Hush. I'm trying to listen!

WHOA.

What?

THAT'S MY HEAD UP THERE. OR, IT WAS FOR AN EVENING. DIDN'T KNOW HE'D DECIDED TO MOUNT IT LIKE A HUNTING TROPHY.

How did you not know that? Aren't you supposed to be everywhere at once?

THINK ABOUT WHAT YOU JUST SAID. THAT'S IMPOSSIBLE.

But how do you manage everything all over the world at once?

IT'S CALLED MULTITASKING.

Is that not the same?

OF COURSE NOT.

Jess shook her head to regain control so that she could continue focusing on Jimmy.

"When I finally told the old woman with the gun that I came in the name of the Lord, she could see the power that emanated from my person, and even a sinful, slop-eating pig like her could tell that she was no match for me when I had His Word behind me."

That doesn't sound like granny. Well, the gun does.

DON'T WORRY, HE'S COMPLETELY FULL OF SHIT. EXCEPT FOR THE GUN. THAT PART IS TRUE.

"The old hag let me through, and that's when I saw the truth of God's message. Before me was a woman on all fours—an unwed mother—grunting and cursing, bringing another sinner into this world, and it became so clear to me just how far we *haven't* come since God put us on this earth. We're still such vile beasts. Maybe we didn't used to be, but now, in this age of science and technology and philosophy, we're no better than pigs. *Sumus omnes porcos*—we are all pigs. *Sed Deus est Aper*—but God is the Hog."

ME DAMN IT.

Is that really how it went the night I was born?

IT BASICALLY IS, BUT HE HAS THE MEANING WRONG.

Why did you come to him as a hog?

BECAUSE NO ONE SWERVES FOR DEER.

While she wasn't quite sure how swerving played into it, she now understood that Jimmy was a two-faced liar.

Either that or Ice Cream Jimmy really *did* have a brother who looked just like him and pretended to be a reverend.

Jimmy lifted his arms toward the congregation. "And as we rolleth in our own filth, let us not forget who it was that maketh this same filth."

And in unison the congregation replied. "It was us who maketh this filth that we now rolleth in like good little piggies but sinners all."

Jess's head jerked around to look at the older woman sitting next to her who had just spoken along with the rest of the room. How did they all know what to say? What did any of that even mean?

And then Jimmy responded with, "And as we are pigs, God is a Hog."

And then the congregation replied, "Lord I offer my heart as Your slop bucket if it so pleaseth You to fill."

UH. HARD PASS ON THAT.

Jimmy waited until the echo from the crowd's incomprehensible words faded, and then he nodded solemnly and steepled his fingers over his mouth for a moment before speaking again. "Now, the child that was born that night, the embodiment of our Original Sin, was a little baby girl." As an aside behind his hand he added, "Naturally," and winked at the crowd, who laughed.

Why are they laughing?

THERE WAS SOME SLOPPY TRANSLATION WORK A WHILE BACK, AND … DON'T WORRY ABOUT IT.

What's Original Sin?

IT WAS A TERRIBLE IDEA IS WHAT IT WAS. I WAS

BORED. IT'S HARD NOT TO BE WHEN YOU CONTROL EVERYTHING.

Uh, this doesn't sound good …

IT'S REALLY NOT. I THOUGHT I'D SPICE THINGS UP WITH SOME CONFLICT. SO I GAVE UP A LITTLE CONTROL AND CREATED IMPERFECTION. THINGS HAVE BEEN SPIRALING DOWNWARD EVER SINCE.

That's what Original Sin is? Imperfection?

BASICALLY. BUT IT'S MORE LIKE ORIGINAL MISTAKE, AND ONE I'VE BEEN TRYING TO FIX FOR, OH, EVER.

Is that why there are so many earthquakes in Asia?

BINGO.

And am I the embodiment of Original Mistake?

NO. WELL KIND OF, BUT EVERYONE IS.

"Our all-powerful God had given me all the signs I needed to understand Him, because He knows that our poor, animalistic, hubristic brains will only listen to wisdom if we feel like we've thought of it ourselves."

Are you really all-powerful?

SEE? TRANSLATION. IT WAS SUPPOSED TO BE "POWERFUL AND ALL THAT" NOT "ALL POWERFUL."

"To mark this joyous day in our church's history, I have two special guests. They've refused the call for years, but God has brought them to us now as a gift to me for my unwavering service to Him."

A knot formed in Jessica's stomach. *This* wasn't fair. Jimmy had just spent the past ten minutes making her and her mother out to be hardly more than animals, and now he was going to draw attention to them? It was cruel. All she wanted was to be able to continue liking Jimmy Dean, but he was making that extremely difficult.

"Destinee and Jessica, would you please stand?"

Destinee's hand flew over to Jess's thigh and gripped it hard to keep her sitting. Taking the lead from her mother, Jess played dumb as well.

"Come now," Jimmy prompted, smiling in a way that didn't make any sense in Jess's mind. "Stand! Don't be shy!" He gestured in their direction, and all those around them started to look left, right, behind. So Destinee did the same, and Jessica followed suit.

"That one! The one in the red shirt!" It wasn't Jimmy who called her out, but Trent Wurst. Jess felt like smiting the boy but didn't think that would help convince people she wasn't the embodiment of sin.

DO YOU WANT ME TO SMITE HIM?

No! They'll think it's me! I have to face him and his stupid sister in school tomorrow!

TRUE. AND A GOOD, SOLID SMITING CAN GET PRETTY MESSY.

Finally, once everyone in their vicinity was locked onto Jessica and Destinee, there was no real choice left but to stand. Maybe it wouldn't be so bad after all.

"Wonderful! Let's all give them a round of applause for embracing their filthy, sloppy sin."

Or maybe it would be.

"I don't—" Destinee started to protest, but she was drowned out by the applause.

"Come up here!" Jimmy said, waving them toward him animatedly. "Come! Come!"

Destinee's eyes were locked onto him, and Jess was fairly certain that if her mother had the power to smite, Jimmy would already be a mess of blood, guts, and white fabric on the stage.

As she followed a step behind her mother down the aisle between the pews, Jess could feel hundreds of eyes glued to her. She didn't like it one bit.

Destinee turned back to Jess. "Stay behind me," she murmured. "And don't let him get to you. We'll get through this, baby."

The walk up to the altar seemed longer than the track Jess had to run in PE every day. Eyes followed them, and Jess kept hers glued to the back of her mother's shirt.

I changed my mind. Smite them all.

IT'S TEMPTING, BUT I HAVE A BETTER IDEA. I NEED YOU TO PAY ATTENTION.

Images began flashing through her mind with the same vivid detail as when she'd first seen Mr. Wurst and Ms. Rickles naked-wrestling in kindergarten. The images flowed slowly at first, then more rapidly, but she was somehow able to recall each and every one like a memory stored in her mind. The first image didn't quite make sense to her—it showed Jimmy and a teenaged girl talking close and in low tones—then there was Jimmy in a barn with teenage girls huddled nearby, then God was a hog, then there was her house, then there was her mother giving birth ...

The images started to create a cohesive narrative as she finally reached the steps to the stage. Not only was Jimmy a liar, he was a big, fat liar, and she felt the betrayal of their ice cream dates acutely.

Jimmy grabbed a handheld microphone from the lectern and emphatically motioned Destinee and Jessica closer to him.

Murmuring had begun to rise up from the congregation, but he put a swift end to it as soon as he raised a finger to his lips. "I see some of you think it wise to gossip and judge these two, but do not! While they may represent the worst of our kind, there is a little bit of them in all of us."

JUST LIKE THERE'S BEEN A LITTLE BIT OF JIMMY IN MOST OF THE WOMEN IN THIS CHURCH ...

Huh?

"Instead of judging them, we should be thanking them. If it weren't for Destinee and her swinelike but *fully human* daughter, none of us would be here in this church today, trying so very hard to wash ourselves clean, while admitting that the task is impossible for us. We are all pigs, and we know that now, thanks to these two. Through their filth, we are able to seek purification." He snorted loudly. "Praise God!" The rest of the church snorted back.

Then Jimmy bowed his head, and Jess wondered if he was thinking or if God had finally decided to give him a stroke. She hoped for the latter.

Suddenly his head shot up, and he yelled, "Praise God! For He has just spoken to me!"

NOT TRUE. OOO ... SO NOT TRUE.

"And He told me that these two have been brought here to be cleansed! For if they can be cleansed, then *anyone* can be cleansed."

Jess felt the bones in her hand grind together under her mother's crushing grip.

"Come forth, you human sows, and tell us your sins! Confess and you shall be cleansed." Jimmy extended out the handheld microphone toward Destinee. Destinee's nostrils flared and her lips thinned, the crevice between them shortening, the skin around them turning white, and as she reached for the mic, Jess squeezed her hand hard before intercepting it. She looked up at her mother and tried to give a meaningful glance. There wasn't another way she could communicate that she might actually know what she was doing. Destinee raised her eyebrows and Jess nodded.

"'Bout time he showed up," Destinee mumbled.

"Oh!" Jimmy exclaimed. "Looks like this little lady is eager to be cleansed! Go on then, Jessica. Tell us your sins."

He folded his hands in front of him, smiling at her encouragingly, almost warmly. It was clear he thought he'd won, that she'd be too embarrassed to disagree with him and too eager to be liked and accepted to speak the truth that they both knew. She looked him in the eyes and returned the smile. He took a step back to give her the stage.

That step back was a mistake, old man.

Then she turned to the large congregation. Oh holy cow there were a lot of people. Her heart leaped into her throat at the sight of so many faces turned toward her, waiting patiently for her to speak. They were looking to her for hope, hope that their sins could be washed away.

I can't do this.

OF COURSE YOU CAN. IT'S GOING TO BE AWESOME. TRUST ME. I KNOW A THING OR TWO ABOUT AWE.

She looked back over her shoulder again where Jimmy appeared more confident than ever that she was about to do his bidding. Why was he doing this to her? Why couldn't he just stay her friend? Maybe she could go along with it for now and then talk with him after to convince him he should change his mind. Maybe telling this crowd of nine hundred and sixty people that she was who Jimmy said she was wouldn't be so bad.

But when her eyes shifted over to land on her mother, there was really no decision to be made. She knew what she needed to do next. She turned back to the crowd.

"My name is Jessica McCloud. Jimmy Dean showed up at my house the night I was born, and yes, he was sent by God Himself." That pleased the congregation, and a handful of the members nodded in approval. Then her eyes landed on the Wursts. It looked like Christmas had come early for Courtney and Trent, and even from this distance, she could tell they were holding their breath for what came next, expecting this to be the best week of school ever.

CHRISTMAS HAS COME EARLY, BITCHES, BUT NOT LIKE YOU—

Get out of my thoughts!

"But the message he was sent to deliver is that I'm the daughter of God."

The room was still silent. Did no one hear what she'd just said? A handful of seconds passed before she spotted the first signs of confusion.

THEY THINK YOU'RE BEING METAPHORICAL.

She wasn't completely sure what that meant, but she clarified anyway, "I'm not being metaphorical."

YOU'RE LITERALLY MY DAUGHTER.

"I'm literally God's daughter."

Murmuring rose up from the crowd, but God wasn't yet satisfied.

I MADE SWEET, GRITTY LOVE TO DESTINEE, AND THEN NINE MONTHS LATER YOU WERE BORN.

"God made sweet, gritty love to Destinee and then …" but she could tell from the shouts of outrage that whatever "sweet, gritty love" was, it was something that people didn't talk about in church.

She had to shout above the noisy crowd to continue making her point. "Your reverend is a complete fraud." A hand grabbed hers on the mic, and she looked up to see Jimmy bearing down on her as he struggled to wrest it from her grip. She fought against him. "He's twisted the message of God and—"

When she felt sharp nails dig into the back of her hand, cutting through the persistent tingling in her skin, she yelped and the mic popped free. He stepped in front of her to regain control of the masses. "Ha! What lies! Your sin knows no end! If you really *are* the daughter of God, prove it."

"But you didn't have to prove anything," she said, though no one except Jimmy, Destinee, and perhaps the front row could hear her without amplification.

"Be my guest!" He bowed demonstratively, his arm outstretched toward the crowd. "Prove to us that you're the daughter of God Himself, rather than an abomination, the physical manifestation of our Original Sin, a reminder to all that we are nothing more than pigs on this earth."

"I—I don't know how to prove it. It just is." The only thing she knew to do that wasn't perfectly human was smiting, but she doubted making a human explode at that point in time would do much to help bring people over to her side of things.

These people will believe whatever they want to believe. I can't prove anything to them, other than the fact that I'm bad.

NOW YOU'RE GETTING IT. BUT DON'T WORRY, THE SEED HAS BEEN PLANTED.

"I see. Nothing to back up your claim." Jimmy shook his head sadly.

Destinee had had enough. She took two steps forward and grabbed Jimmy by his perfectly styled hair, holding his head still so she could lean in and use the mic on his headset. "This is some bullshit. Psychos like y'all were the ones who nailed Jesus to the cross, and I'll be damned if I let my baby girl go the same way."

Jimmy pulled his head free of her grip, but she wasn't done. Jess knew all too well how Destinee's voice could travel when she was angry.

"And what the hell is this shit?" she shrieked, pointing to the long, metal tubs propped up on the floor next to the stage. Jess hadn't even noticed them until her mother pointed them out. "Are those *troughs*? What the hell kind of a messenger from God builds troughs in his church?"

Jimmy remained calm, though. "A pig deserves a trough. It is not our fault that you don't understand the rites of communion with *Deus Aper*."

She looked like she was about to say something else to the congregation, then paused and turned to Jimmy, squinting at him. And when she spoke, it was the way one friend might speak to another. "That is some fucked-up shit, Jimmy."

AMEN.

Jimmy clutched at his heart. "Listen to the way she blasphemes at the altar! But we shalt not condemn her for being disgusting, because we are all disgusting, each and every one of us, even if she is slightly more disgusting."

"Come on, Jess." Destinee grabbed her daughter's hand and led her down the stairs so quickly that Jess almost missed one, but caught herself before she fell, which would have been the only way to make this whole morning even more embarrassing.

"Look at how they flee when confronted with their sins!" Jimmy called after them.

Jess couldn't get out of there quick enough. She would have run, but that was a show of fear that even the dumbest predator in the animal kingdom would have recognized.

This is the longest aisle in the world!

"Let us pray for them. Please bow your heads. Lord, Heavenly Father, you created us in your image, and we have all failed you, devolved into swine so that the only way we can recognize Your presence is when You descend to our level. Thank you, God, for taking the body of a Hog to remind us of Your mercy and willingness to meet us where we are so that we may strive to rise up to the greatness we hold inside us, locked away behind layer and layer of sinful lard ..."

"Motherfucker," Destinee spat, picking up the pace so that Jess was left with the choice of jogging or being dragged. She chose jogging.

"... And when we eat this blessed bacon, a food that You've definitely changed Your mind about since Leviticus, let us be reminded of Your glory."

Only a few more feet to the doors, then it would be a quick trip through the foyer, under the arch, through the parking lot, and into the relative safety of their Nissan. Jess focused her mind on that to escape the present, which was becoming more unfathomable by the second. The last thing she heard before they made it into the foyer left her wishing she'd never met Jimmy Dean at all—not even Ice Cream Jimmy.

His voice felt like it was chasing them out the door. "In Your holy name we pray. *Sooie!*"

And the congregation replied, "*Sooie!*"

Chapter Eight

Destinee and Jessica agreed to cross church off their list of possible mother–daughter activities. But that didn't make the humiliation of it stop rattling around in Jess's head, even long after they'd returned to Mooretown. Destinee didn't seem any less upset about it than Jess was. In fact, she seemed even angrier about her daughter being called the embodiment of Original Sin than Jess was about being called the embodiment of Original Sin.

The car ride home from Midland had been silent except for the radio crooning soft country hits, and Jess was grateful for the time to think without either of her parents speaking. When a commercial for White Light Church came on the radio, Destinee punched the dial repeatedly until the car was completely silent, which Jess didn't mind so much either.

But once they arrived home, Destinee set her purse down on the coffee table and headed straight into her bedroom, closing the door before leaving Jimmy a loud, lengthy voicemail that Jess could tell was only the tip of the rageberg.

For dinner that night, Destinee prepared handmade mashed potatoes, mashed carrots, which seemed like a strange way to prepare carrots, and the most tenderized flank stake Jess had ever tried. The prep time was about forty-five minutes of screaming and pounding, gnashing and mashing, during which Jess stayed hidden away in her room, trying to take her mind off of life with a TV show about deep-sea predators.

When she was finally called to the table, Jess wasn't sure what to say to her mother and was fairly certain nothing would quell the anger that bubbled just under the surface, breaking through here and there with a heavy sigh or a grunt. So Jessica ate her dinner quietly. She wished that the humiliation they'd shared could have united them instead of making things feel so stiff, but that wasn't how it turned out. She wondered why. After dinner she finished up her personal essay for language arts (*Prompt: Talk about a time when you learned a lesson the hard way*) before falling asleep to the soothing and paternal voice of David Attenborough as he narrated life's ability to adapt and evolve in the old *The Living Planet VHSs* Destinee had kept from her childhood.

The next morning, Jess awoke feeling like she'd nabbed all of twenty minutes of actual sleep. Her mind wasn't anywhere near ready to let go of the electric anxiety that pinballed in her skull. School could have been a much-needed distraction, except she knew better than to hope for that. Trent and Courtney would be there, and the thought of their snide gloating and prodding made her nauseated.

At least I'll get to see Miranda first and tell her what happened.

There were times when Jess had lamented only having one close friend, but right now she knew it was better than nothing. In fact, it was everything.

She'd had gotten in a habit of walking to school each morning and, as she dressed, she mentally prepared for the journey that would involve putting one foot in front of the other, over and over again. It seemed like a tall order, considering. But at breakfast, Destinee poured herself a glass of orange juice, then one for Jess, and sat at the table facing her daughter.

"You look the way I feel. Let me drive you this morning."

"Okay."

They sipped their juice in silence, then Destinee stood. "I guess I should put on pants."

As they pulled into the drop-off loop of Mooreson Elementary, Destinee broke the tired silence again. "This is a small town, Jess. I reckon there's a good chance some of those asshats in Midland yesterday were from here."

"They were. I recognized some."

Destinee shut her eyes and took a deep breath. "Damn. Who was it?"

"The Wursts."

"Ruth was there?!"

Was that their mother's name? She couldn't recall. "I just know Courtney and Trent."

"Father the police chief?"

Jess nodded.

A small growl escaped from the depth of Destinee's chest. "Yeah, that'll be Ruth then. I must've been too wrapped up in Jimmy's bullshit to notice her. Damn. Ruth Wurst. Damn.

"Well, word definitely will've gotten out." She put the car into park and grabbed Jess's head, turning it toward her to look into her daughter's eyes. "You don't take shit from anyone, you hear me? You're God's daughter. His son might've lacked a backbone in the end, but I didn't raise you that way. Don't take shit from *anyone*. Do what you gotta do. You may get in trouble with the school, but you won't be in trouble at home, you hear?"

Jess nodded.

"Good." Destinee leaned forward and kissed her on the forehead. "Love you, baby."

"Love you, too."

She hopped out of the car, feeling a little better than when she'd left the house. She was ready to find Miranda immediately and fill her in, maybe even talk a little trash to get herself worked up.

But as it would happen (and from her recent interactions with God, she guessed this to be more of a chance thing than a divine plan thing), she didn't get three steps into the front door of the school before she ran into the last two people she wanted to see.

They were gathered in a small group of kids, talking quietly, and when they spotted Jessica, they stopped, looked at her with their noses up, then turned back to the group and started laughing. She wanted to tell off the

Wursts, but she didn't know how since they hadn't actually said anything to her. Her resolve melted away before it even existed, and she hurried off to find Miranda.

When she walked into her classroom, though, Miranda wasn't there yet. Thankfully, Mrs. Thomas was.

God bless Mrs. Thomas.

As luck would have it, the woman had been shuffled around from one grade level to the next each year, so that Jessica had ended up having her for kindergarten, first, third, and now sixth. While the grade levels had been selected for Mrs. Thomas by the administration, the teacher had flat-out told Jessica that she'd been allowed to pick most of the students on her roster. Jessica, she said, had been her top pick. Miranda had also made the list, and Jess often wondered if Trent and Courtney were selected by Mrs. Thomas or if she was forced to take them on because of the "politics" she often mentioned.

Jess cleared her throat as she entered the classroom to make her presence known.

Mrs. Thomas looked up from where she sat at her desk, and her sweet singsongy voice greeted Jess like a warm hug. "Good morning, Miss McCloud! How was your weekend?"

"Not great." Jess set her stuff down at one of the front desks. There were already a couple of students in the room, but they hung out in the back, as far away from the teacher as they could. They didn't even realize how lucky they were to be in Mrs. Thomas's class. Ingrates.

"You want to talk about it?" The warm, dulcet tone of her voice almost made Jess agree. Almost.

"Not really."

"If you change your mind, you know you can always talk to me about it, okay?"

Jess smiled. She couldn't help it. "Yeah, okay, thanks."

She took her seat at the front of the class, keeping her eyes forward as the rest of her classmates slowly filed in.

Trent, at least, had learned a healthy fear of Mrs. Thomas, meaning he knew better than to antagonize Jess when she was sitting only feet from the teacher's desk. He claimed his usual desk, midway back and against the window.

Courtney, being a more subtle, skilled tormentor, forewent her usual spot in the very middle of the classroom —where she was able to monitor the joy levels of her classmates most effectively and was thereby able to nip anyone's attempt at enthusiasm or fun right in the bud with a sharp, shaming verbal prod, never more than a single sentence because it never had to be—and planted herself a single row back from the front, directly behind Jessica's desk.

But Courtney only managed to cough a few insults throughout the morning without Mrs. Thomas noticing. The brat also managed a handful of well-timed snorting sounds that earned her muffled giggles from her classmates and a confused side eye from Mrs. Thomas, but as that was the worst Jess had to endure for the first half of the day, she wasn't complaining. Sure it was terrible, but Jessica had her own scale of terribleness, one that had registered higher levels of terribleness than most children her age knew possible. Courtney's meager attempts at bullying rated quite low in *terribles* (the unit of measurement for her scale).

In fact, Jessica's dark mood from that morning had brightened by lunchtime. If snorting was the worst of it, maybe she could make it through the day after all. Especially when she knew Mrs. Thomas had her back if things got out of hand.

It also helped to know that if things got *especially* brutal, she could do what she needed to survive without worrying about her mother doubling any punishment. A little support went a long way, it seemed.

And speaking of support, since Miranda had shown up to school ten minutes after the start of class, not only did she miss all the juicy gossip floating around the hall, Jess wasn't able to vent to her until lunchtime. But once Miranda had gotten her tray from the lunch line and sat across from Jess at the end of the small table off to the side in the cafeteria, Jessica let loose with a torrent of information. Sometimes it bothered her that there weren't others who wanted to regularly sit by her and Miranda, but she appreciated the privacy now that she had something important to talk about that she didn't want others to overhear.

"Ohhh," Miranda said, once Jess had filled her in completely and then some. "Now it makes a lot more sense why Courtney wouldn't stop coughing."

"Yep."

"I guess that also explains why she was snorting."

"That's the worst part!" Jess exclaimed before catching herself and lowering the volume to an enthusiastic whisper.

"Why were *they* snorting at *me*? They're the ones who take communion from a trough! *I* should've been snorting at *them!*"

Miranda struggled with her milk carton, but eventually opened it and asked, "Then why didn't you?" before taking a sip.

Jess sighed. "I don't know."

"Think about it. If you have to act like a pig to make fun of someone, you might not be great at making fun of people."

Miranda had a way of putting things that helped keep Jess on an even keel, and this was no exception. Her ability to see through all the garbage seemed like a superpower to Jess, whose life sometimes felt like nothing *but* the garbage. "Yeah, I guess you're right." She chuckled. "Did you see Courtney's face when she did it? She went a little cross-eyed."

They both broke into giggles, drawing the attention of the girls at the table next to them, who Jess could have sworn were too busy taking selfies of themselves to notice anything else.

Sandra Thomas was among the gaggle. "What is it?" she asked abrasively, looking demandingly from Jess to Miranda but sounding self-conscious. Her phone was still extended at arm's length, directed at herself even as she spoke to them.

"Nothing." Miranda waved her off. "You look great. That's a good angle for you. Makes you look like you have boobs."

Sandra smiled. "Thanks!" She puckered up at Miranda

and held that pose for a few seconds longer than socially comfortable. She looked at her phone. "Perfect. Chris is going to love that." She turned the screen toward Stephanie Lee—the only Asian in all of Mooreson Elementary—who never went anywhere without her flip phone, her sparkly belt, or Sandra.

"Oh my god!" Stephanie exclaimed. "You look so hot! Chris is going to die when he sees that. Oh my god, you're so lucky you're pretty. I wish I had your hair." Stephanie tousled hers to give it volume, puckered up, and took a few more pixilated selfies.

Jess turned back to her best friend, who was doing an admirable job of pretending not to have heard anything about Sandra's new boyfriend as she shoveled a lump of mashed potatoes into her mouth.

"Hey," Jess said, leaning forward and speaking so she wouldn't be overheard. "You're way prettier than Sandra."

Miranda rolled her eyes, but even with a mouth full of instapotato she couldn't hide the smile that forced its way to the surface. A few starchy particles shot out of her mouth as she begrudgingly replied, "Thanks."

Chapter Nine

_____

Math class had been a source of stress for Jessica all year. Not because she found it difficult, though. Math was her strongest subject by a mile, and that was precisely why it had become a source of anxiety. The fact that it happened right after lunch only added a layer of indigestion to the whole ordeal, which mostly consisted of a constant struggle between getting good grades and not letting anyone else in the class know she was getting good grades.

Something had shifted during the summer between fifth and sixth grade, and being at the top of the class went from being a way to earn respect to the fastest way to draw a target on your back. When Jess had mentioned her observation to her mother, Destinee nodded sympathetically before explaining that it would only get worse once Jess graduated into Marymoore Junior High the following year, meaning now was the time to practice dealing with it.

So even though Trent and Courtney had been

manageable in their teasing leading up to lunch, Jess knew better than to assume that she was in the clear. There was *nothing* that Trent and Courtney enjoyed more than bragging about their grades, and for some reason, no one ever tried to tease *them* for it.

Then, to make matters worse, Mrs. Thomas started class with, "I've graded all your tests from last Friday, so I'll hand those back to you now."

Jess's heart sank into her gut. She'd forgotten about the test last Friday. She'd studied for it, like she always did for tests, but not *that* much. It was just geometry, and God had made it pretty simple. Everything came down to 360 degrees. She wasn't sure why so many people seemed to struggle with it.

I TRIED TO THROW EVERYONE A SLOW PITCH ON THIS ONE BECAUSE I FELT BAD ABOUT QUANTUM PHYSICS, He'd told her.

Mrs. Thomas settled down the class and began handing back the graded geometry tests.

Did she want a good grade or not? She couldn't decide.

Mrs. Thomas leaned over and smiled at Jess as she sat the test face down on her desk. "Great work." She winked.

Jess flipped over the paper. A *105* was written in red pen and circled. She'd aced it and nailed the extra credit.

"What'd you get?" Miranda asked, leaning over.

Jess glanced casually over her shoulder at Courtney and Trent to make sure they weren't paying attention before she whispered, "A hundred and five." She'd never felt greater dread about getting so high a grade.

"Nice!" beamed. "Maybe you can help me with my corrections. I only got a seventy-eight."

"Oh my god," Courtney said from behind them. "You only got a seventy-eight? This was, like, the easiest test ever."

Miranda turned in her seat to wrinkle her nose at Courtney. "Oh yeah? What'd you get?"

"Please. Both Trent and I got a hundred and one."

So many emotions flooded Jess's brain at once. Satisfaction that she'd beaten them both, disgust at their smugness, anger for Courtney's insult to Miranda. She could feel it intensify in a whirlwind inside her like a chemical reaction releasing fumes that built up in her chest. Jessica couldn't take it. She knew that if she didn't release some of the pressure, this could end in a smiting. She turned in her chair. "Oh wow! That's amazing! Yet *another* test where you both get the exact same score. Huh. Interesting."

Trent looked at her like someone had shoved a dirty diaper under his nose. "What are you getting at? We're twins. That happens."

"True," Jessica conceded disingenuously. "Especially if you both cheat on every single test."

"You're just bitter because we always get the best grades in the class," Courtney said, but her face was turning red.

"Not this time!" Miranda said victoriously. Jess inhaled sharply as a reflex. "Jess beat you."

Miranda had gone and done it again without meaning to. She'd betrayed Jess to her tormentors. It was impossible to be mad at her, though, because Miranda never meant to set her up like this.

"She got a hundred and five," Miranda finished, smirking and still unaware of the damage she'd done.

A momentary look of panic surfaced in Trent's eyes before he tamped it down. "That's only because *she* cheats."

"I do not!"

"Of course you do," Courtney said, picking up where her brother left off. "Why wouldn't you? The Reverend Dean said you're the Antichrist. And the Antichrist would definitely cheat."

"Jimmy never called me that!" Jess protested. At least she didn't remember him saying it, but it could have happened once she and her mom had fled the service. She also wasn't sure what exactly "Antichrist" meant, but judging by the fact that it was coming from Courtney's forked tongue, it couldn't be good.

"Yes, he did. He said it to my mom after church yesterday and she told us. He said you're the Antichrist and as punishment for mimicking the Holy Son, you won't live a day longer than he did!"

"Yeah!" Trent chimed in. "Jesus will kill you dead!"

Mrs. Thomas, who was returning to her desk after handing out the last of the graded papers, perked up at the word Jesus being shouted in a public school and turned quickly on her heels, swooping down on Trent, despite it being Courtney who was the pack leader of the hunt.

Jess could almost feel the waves of anger radiating from her teacher as the woman breezed past Jess's desk to stand less than a foot away from Trent. "Excuse me, Mr. Wurst? I could swear I just heard you trying to shame another person *in my classroom* for their beliefs. Did I hear that correctly?" The thin thread of sweetness she'd woven into her words only served to halt all activity in the classroom in an instant.

When Mrs. Thomas was upset with a student, she laid it out plain, no emotion, no sugar-coating at all. But when Mrs. Thomas was furious with a student, well, it sounded exactly like this.

Trent's eyes were giant saucers, the blue of them overrun by the expanding black holes of his pupils. "No, ma'am," he said innocently, his voice wavering.

Wracking her brain for a time when Mrs. Thomas had ever looked this angry, Jess came up empty-handed. The teacher stood, one hand on her hip, one on her forehead, staring daggers at Trent without speaking, and Jess wondered if anyone else in the room was able to breathe during it, because she certainly wasn't.

"Need I remind you of our previous conversations, Mr. Wurst?"

Trent squinted, appearing lost for only a moment before a memory seemed to surface, and his eyes shot open again. He shook his head.

"You know what?" Mrs. Thomas said. "Go see Principal Finnegan. I've just about had it with your attitude today. You, too, Courtney. I'll be calling your mother after class. And plan on lunch detention for the rest of the week."

They started to protest loudly, but Mrs. Thomas smacked Trent's desk with a flat palm. "No!" That put a stop to it ... and caused everyone in the classroom to jump.

"Go. Now. I'm calling Principal Finnegan to let him know to expect you."

Mrs. Thomas planted herself between Miranda's and Jess's desks, creating what felt like a protective force field around them.

Trent and Courtney gathered up their things and sulked out of the classroom. Watching them slink in shame brought Jess only mild satisfaction. This could've been a highlight of her year if it'd happened any week prior to this one, but now nothing short of watching them flee the classroom with jeers and judgment hot on their heels would have felt like a victory.

Besides, the damage had already been done by their words, and Jess knew this queasy feeling wouldn't go away until she could at least figure out what an Antichrist was. And that would have to wait till later because she was *not* about to ask Mrs. Thomas anything related to religion when the woman was still so red-faced and flustered.

IF IT'S ANY CONSOLATION, MRS. WURST AND JIMMY HAVE BEEN KNOCKING BOOTS FOR ABOUT THREE YEARS NOW.

I don't know what that means. Shut up. Leave me alone.

The last person she wanted to hear from was God, who was solely responsible for every individual misery, both large and small, that she could count in her short life.

Chapter Ten

Even with the Wurst twins in the principal's office for the rest of the afternoon, the end of the school day couldn't come fast enough. As she walked down the crowded hallway, a step behind Miranda, she wondered vaguely what her bed was up to just then. Particularly, what the small, dark, cozy space between her soft cotton sheets and her heavy comforter were up to. She decided she would find out in person as soon as she arrived home, and that plan felt like salve over her raw nerves.

After she waved goodbye to Miranda and just as she hit the pavement on her walk home, she spotted her mother's Nissan pulling into the parent pick-up line a little ways down the block. Even better. She'd be curled up in bed, bathing in the glow of her TV before she knew it.

She climbed into the front passenger's seat, chucked her backpack behind her, and buckled herself in.

Destinee watched and waited until she was settled in to

pull out of line and onto the road. "Thought I'd pick you up in case your day wasn't fantastic."

"Thanks," Jess mumbled.

"So how was it?"

"It wasn't fantastic." She sighed and stared out the window at the redbrick building that had functioned as her prison for the day.

"Mrs. Thomas sent me a text saying you and the Wurst twins had it out. What'd those twerps say?"

"Nothing."

Destinee might be acting sweet, soft, and concerned now, but Jess hadn't forgotten the mashed carrots from the night before. There was no reason why her mother *wouldn't* still be spring-loaded for rage.

"Did you at least stand up for yourself?"

"When I could."

Destinee nodded. "Good."

They made it to the end of the block and were waiting for the next car to go at a stop sign when Jess asked, "How old did Jesus live to be?" as casually as she could manage. People asked those sorts of things all the time, right?

There was a low rumbling sound from deep within Destinee's throat before she inhaled deeply, turned to get a good look at her daughter, and responded, "I think it was thirty-three." Her eyes narrowed. "Why?"

That seemed old enough, but then she realized it was only a handful of years beyond her mother's current age, and suddenly it didn't seem nearly old enough to have to worry about dying. "Just wondering." She considered letting the topic drop, but curiosity burned in her esophagus.

She decided to press her luck. "He was murdered, right?"

"Yeah. Straight up. Cold blooded." Destinee paused, pressed her lips together momentarily. "Baby, why are you asking?"

"No reason. Just wondering." Killed at thirty-three. For everyone else's sins, no less. That seemed like a raw deal, but who was she to say? While she'd long suspected his death was a result of being framed for crimes he didn't commit, it was also possible that he deserved it. Maybe he was a bully and maybe people got tired of it and decided to take him out. She'd never met the guy, even though he was family.

But regardless, if he had been murdered at thirty-three, it shouldn't be hard to outlive him. All she had to do was be sure no one wanted to frame her or kill her. That was simple enough. She had to become less killable.

So, as the Nissan pulled onto the farm-to-market road leading home, Jess brainstormed ways to make herself less killable. Most of her ploys required making more friends, and in that respect, the simple task became herculean.

But something else was still nagging at her. "Mom, what's the Antichrist?"

"What the fuck." Destinee swerved onto the shoulder, the tires kicking up gravel, and threw the car into park. "Why are you asking me this, Jess? The truth, please." Destinee tilted her head forward, waiting impatiently. There was no way to lie when Destinee became this serious. "I'm not mad at you, baby. I just want to know where you heard that word."

"Trent. He said his mother told him that I'm the Antichrist."

Jess worried her mother might be about to pass out as her eyes glazed over slowly and her gaze floated upward to the unoccupied space above Jess's head. Still staring vaguely into nothing, she nodded. "Okay."

Nope. Jess knew not to trust that. Maybe some other lucky kid's mother would say, "Okay" like that and mean it, but there was no universe in which Jess could imagine her mother letting this be. And yet, Destinee appeared calm.

Jess had never been more terrified of what her mother might do.

Destinee glanced over her shoulder at the road, jammed the car into drive, checked her mirrors, and then pulled a U-turn and headed back in the other direction.

"Where are we going?" Ooh, this wasn't going to end well. Destinee was a new kind of angry, a calm and silent kind, which was uncharted territory.

"You're not the Antichrist, Jess. If anyone's the Antichrist, it's Jimmy."

So the Antichrist *was* something bad. Was the Antichrist like the Devil? Yet again, she wondered if Jimmy could be the Devil, and while there was a chance, it didn't feel right. If God had come straight out and said that Jimmy was a *demon*, she could *maybe* get on board with that, even though she'd ruled it out herself. But there was something about him that didn't quite fit with being evil incarnate, an ineptitude that lurked in the shadows of his larger-than-life persona.

Sure, she couldn't officially cross him off of her old Devil List, but there were plenty of people she couldn't rule out based on her one hint of the Devil being born outside of Mooretown. That left her with only one tool to work with: gut instinct.

So the Devil List had become The Unofficial Devil Test, which consisted of asking herself, "Is he/she the Devil?" and waiting to see if a clear "Yes" followed in God-only-knew (literally) what form.

She ran the test every time someone was mean to her, hoping for a positive result, something that just clicked, that "a-ha!" moment where it was so obvious that, *Yes, this person is the Devil*. Once she'd received that result, she could plan on avoiding said person and resume her life with one less dire mystery hanging nebulously overhead.

But so far, the results of The Unofficial Devil Test for each non-native Mooretowner she'd tried it on had come back inconclusive. Well, no, that wasn't quite right. There were three exceptions, three non-natives who Jessica was sure were *not* the Devil. She didn't even need to run the Devil test to know. It was just that obvious.

Firstly, there was Miranda, who was born and spent the first few weeks of her life in Austin until her mother moved back to Mooretown. Then, of course, there was Mrs. Thomas, who frequently mentioned how she was from Louisiana but left as soon as she could and ended up in town after she married Congressman Thomas. Lastly, there was Jessica's neighbor Todd, who always stopped to let her pet his bloodhound, Sampson, when they passed the McCloud home on walks. Todd was too insignificant in her life to be the Devil. And the idea of the Devil owning a slobbery hound like Sampson seemed too silly to be possible.

She decided to run Jimmy Dean through the test again.

Is Jimmy Dean the Devil?

God didn't respond, which was to be expected. He never responded when she ran the test on someone. It was the one surefire way she'd found to make sure God stayed silent, actually.

She let the notion of Jimmy being the Devil bounce around in her mind, and as usual, the results came back inconclusive.

Part of that might have been because Jess's mind was preoccupied with solving the riddle of where Destinee could be driving them. She was coming up short on guesses. She'd been on this stretch of road before, but she didn't know of anyone who lived out here.

"Where are we going?" she asked again, but Destinee remained silent. They exited the road into a small neighborhood with houses easily four times the size of the McCloud double-wide. Every house looked basically the same, like big imposing tanks lined up, ready to march on all the smaller homes of Mooretown.

Even when Destinee pulled up to the curb and parked, Jess couldn't figure out what they were doing. She knew she wasn't in trouble with her mother—why would she be? —but she kind of *felt* like she was in trouble.

Then she saw the Wursts' minivan pull into the driveway a house down.

Oh no.

Destinee rolled her neck in small circles, cracked her knuckles.

"Mom, no."

But her mother had already homed in on the Wurst vehicle. "I'm just gonna talk to her, baby. Don't worry."

She left the car and strode determinedly toward the Wurst family. Jess unbuckled so that she could slide down in her seat to be as inconspicuous as possible, providing a counterweight to Destinee's behavior.

As she peeked above the dashboard, she couldn't hear what her mother was saying, but she could see the expression of confusion then disgust on Mrs. Wurst's face after the woman opened her door, spotted, and then *registered* who it was marching toward her where she sat in the minivan.

Destinee didn't waste a moment with conversation before she grabbed Mrs. Wurst by her perfectly styled and hairsprayed bun and dragged her onto the lawn. Both women began hollering, but Jess couldn't make out any distinct words.

Jessica had never actually witnessed Destinee physically assault another human being, but seeing it unfold didn't come as any major surprise. In fact, she was surprised she'd made it to eleven before seeing a display like this.

Out on the manicured lawn, Destinee waited until Mrs. Wurst took a swing at her before really tearing into the woman. That seemed like a smart tactic to Jess. She made a note of it, in case she ever had to beat up a Wurst herself.

Destinee's first punch made contact with Ruth Wurst's stomach. She let go of her hair and the woman fell to the ground in a heap. Destinee stood over Ruth, but she didn't have to wait long before the woman tried to scramble back onto her feet to retaliate. She was hardly onto her knees before Destinee jumped on top of her, flattening her out, and began to deal more blows with less precision than her initial gut punch.

CATFIGHT!

God! Stop her!

YOU KIDDING ME? THIS IS HOT AS HELL. TRUST ME ON THAT. I KNOW.

What?

DO YOU UNDERSTAND HOW MANY TIMES I WISH I COULD SMITE PEOPLE WITHOUT IT BEING ALL OVER THE NEWS? EVERY ME-DAMN DAY. I LOVE IT WHEN PEOPLE TAKE JUSTICE INTO THEIR OWN HANDS.

Mrs. Wurst somehow rallied and freed herself with a firm closed-fist slap to the side of Destinee's head so she could struggle to her knees before Destinee launched another attack.

YOU KNOW, THIS IS WHAT MADE ME FALL FOR YOUR MOTHER.

Her beating someone up?

YEP.

Who?

SAME PERSON.

Wait, my mom has beat up Mrs. Wurst before?!

YEP.

Should I try to break them up?

NAH. JUST ENJOY IT.

I think I should break it up.

THOU SHALT NOT BREAK UP THIS MEGA HOT CATFIGHT!

Jess sighed. If God was into this, then maybe it wasn't so bad. Maybe she should just enjoy the show. God probably wouldn't let anything horrible happen to the mother of His child anyway. Plus, Destinee *did* have a pretty good uppercut.

Pausing from her studious observations, Jessica glanced over at Trent and Courtney, who had gotten out of the minivan and were standing against the car, watching and crying. What worthless babies. Jess sat up straight in her seat and waited until the twins looked at her. Then she smiled and waved.

OH YEAH!

Destinee stood over Mrs. Wurst and delivered a final kick into the woman's butt before wiping her sweaty hair from her face and darting back to the Nissan.

She jumped in and quickly started the engine. "Woo! Hell yeah!"

She was bleeding from the nose and a cut below her right eye. The crimson flow dripped down onto her cobalt-blue pharmacy polo, wicking into expanding mahogany stains. "God damn, baby! That felt so good." She pulled away from the curb and sped down the street, past the rows of tank houses.

"Are you okay?" Jess asked hesitantly, wondering if her mother had officially lost her mind.

"Better than okay. I feel amazing! That bitch had it coming. Should've known better than to go for round two with Destinee McCloud! Woo!" Destinee took a hand off the steering wheel and offered up her palm.

Without meaning to, or expecting to, Jess started to laugh. She high-fived her mother.

TELL HER HOW SEXY I THINK SHE IS.

"No! Gross!"

"Huh?" Destinee asked.

"Nothing."

"Is God talking to you?"

"Yes. He's being gross."

Destinee addressed the roof of the car. "I *knew* you'd like that, you dirty bastard! Ha!" She turned up the radio and played the top of the steering wheel like a bongo while dancing in her seat.

But by the time they'd pulled into their driveway, it seemed that her rush had worn off. She sighed, turned off the car and sat there, looking drained. Her face had swollen up nicely, and Jess wondered what Mrs. Wurst's face looked like right about now. She hoped it looked terrible.

"Cops are probably gonna come looking for me in the next few hours or so," Destinee said. "Shit." She sighed. "Guess I'll call your grandma to come stay, in case I gotta go down to the station to clear some things up." She shook her head somberly. "Dammit. I'll never hear the end of this from Mama."

"Is Mrs. Wurst going to call the cops on you?"

Destinee shrugged a single shoulder. "She doesn't really have to. Her husband's the chief of police, so she just has to tell him, and he'll bring down the hammer. God dammit. Last time she was just banging some roughneck who was only in town two weeks out of every month. Bitch sure did marry up ..."

No, this couldn't be how the world worked. It wasn't fair or just. Beating up Mrs. Wurst was supposed to make things *even*, not land Destinee in jail and Jessica in custody of a grandma she hadn't seen in years and hardly remembered. There had to be a way around it.

Then something prickled in her mind, like a polite tap on the shoulder. She almost didn't tune into it, didn't notice that something might be there. A tiny bit of information that Jess didn't quite understand nagged at her like it could make itself useful.

It could be nothing, but then again, God had said it, so maybe it was important.

"What does 'knocking boots' mean?" she asked.

Destinee was dabbing at her nose in the mirror with a tissue but paused from her clean up, turning slowly to face her daughter. "Why you asking?"

Jess could tell from her mother's cautious tone that her suspicions might be correct. "What does it mean?"

"It means having adult ... um, what's the word? Adult ... ? Shit, my brain's lagging right now. It means fuckin'. Where'd you hear that? Your Daddy teach you that?"

While she still only had a general idea of what fucking meant—mostly gathered from comments she overheard her mother make to friends over the phone about people they knew—Jess had a pretty good feeling about this. She held back a smile but nodded enthusiastically. "Yep. He may've mentioned that Mrs. Wurst and Jimmy Dean had been knocking boots for a few years."

After a moment's pause, a few vacant blinks, Destinee cackled and slapped her knee. "Ha!" She stared ahead at the garage door, a plan clearly formulating. "Ha!" She slapped the steering wheel with both hands. "You're a smart one, Jess. Plotting, but smart." She hurriedly tossed her phone and wallet into her purse. "I have a call to make, and thankfully not to your cranky old grandma."

"Mrs. Wurst?"

Destinee nodded and stepped out of the car. Jess grabbed her backpack and followed. Pausing at the front door, Destinee turned to her daughter. "How do you feel about pizza for dinner?"

"Hell yes!" She couldn't remember the last time they'd ordered pizza on a Monday.

Chapter Eleven

When Jess woke the next morning, the events of the afternoon before didn't seem so grand. The shine had worn off, and now she was facing even bigger problems. Would Trent and Courtney's teasing double? There was no way of knowing, so she resigned herself to finding out the hard way. With any luck, she could use the pointers she picked up from her mom's fight to help her through the day, if need be.

At least Mom won the fight. Jess felt a great deal of pride in that. The Wurst twins were awful, but Jessica's mom could whoop their mom's ass any day of the week.

Each time she thought back to the way Destinee had pulled Mrs. Wurst from her minivan, bun-first, a swell of confidence expanded in Jess's chest. Maybe someday she would have the courage to do something like that to someone who deserved it. It seemed like a better option than smiting, anyway.

As she stepped into the classroom, her eyes

automatically searched for the Wurst twins. But they weren't there yet. Miranda was, though, and greeted her friend the same as always, with a smile and a small wave. Jess couldn't wait to tell her about the fight.

She got two steps into the room before Mrs. Thomas looked up from her seat at the desk, stood, and hurried over, intercepting her before she made it even halfway to Miranda. She let the teacher gently guide her back toward the door, out of earshot of the other students. "Are you okay?" Mrs. Thomas asked with a calm intensity, resting a hand on Jess's shoulder.

Was she okay? Why was her teacher asking that? Did she know about the fight?

Please, of course she did. This was Mooretown. Everyone knew everyone else's business, *especially* when that business involved an ass kicking. "Yeah. I'm fine."

Mrs. Thomas nodded, but based upon her narrowed eyes, she wasn't convinced. "I heard what happened with your mother and Mrs. Wurst."

Jessica repressed a proud smile, momentarily remembering the howling laughter she and Destinee had shared over pizza the evening before after Jessica noticed a few of Ruth Wurst's blonde hairs stuck to Destinee's blue pharmacy shirt. "I'm pretty sure everyone's heard by now."

Mrs. Thomas pressed her lips together tightly, scanning Jessica rapidly from face to feet then back again. "That's Mooretown for you." She paused. Was she concerned that Jessica might have been injured in the scrape? Was she coming to congratulate Jessica on her mother's decisive victory? Or was this about something else entirely, and the mention of the fight was just small talk?

Mrs. Thomas flared her nostrils as she sucked in air. Then she straightened up. "You know, Jessica, I'm aware that Trent and Courtney have not been the nicest to you over the years. I've done my best to monitor and mitigate the situation. I understand that sometimes it feels like disciplining them is not enough, considering the torment they seem intent upon doling out to others—you in particular."

"You and my mom have that in common," Jessica said, grinning.

Mrs. Thomas shut her eyes for a moment as her shoulders hitched slightly toward her jawline. "Your mother and I may share that belief, but I feel obligated to tell you that what your mother did to Mrs. Wurst was absolutely, unequivocally wrong."

Blood rushed to Jessica's head, the pulsation pounding in her ears.

Mrs. Thomas went on. "She should not have taken matters into her own hands in that way. It was brutal, vulgar, and not the stuff upon which a healthy civilization is built."

Each new condemnation of Destinee's heroic actions— or at least that's what they'd seemed to be until a few seconds ago—sent a new splash of ice water down Jessica's spine.

"I know it's tempting to resort to violence," Mrs. Thomas continued, "but that doesn't make it right."

Any argument that Destinee shouldn't have beat the

ever-living crap out of Mrs. Wurst had to be fundamentally flawed. Sure, fighting could've gotten Destinee in trouble with the police if Jess hadn't provided useful blackmail, but even God had been all for the violent confrontation, and it *did* seem only fair.

"However"—Mrs. Thomas's stern expression softened around the mouth, though her eyes retained their intense focus—"I'm sure it was just a heat-of-the-moment decision on your mother's part. We're only human, after all, and sometimes we make mistakes. I'm sure she's properly ashamed of herself for it. Granted, it's not her first offense, but she's smart enough. She knows better, I'm sure. Regardless, I wanted to make sure you knew a fistfight is never the answer to your problems. That behavior is completely unacceptable in an educated society."

Jessica swallowed hard but nodded, feeling the surge of blood begin to drain from her face. Her arms grew heavy. Had all her internal organs doubled in weight? It sure felt like it.

"I'm sorry," Jess said. "I shouldn't have told her about it."

The wrinkles around Mrs. Thomas's eyes smoothed, and her lips parted in surprise. She squatted down to look up into Jessica's face, placing her hands on her student's shoulders. "There's nothing for you to be sorry about," she said, shaking her head slowly. "Your mother's irrational and risky behavior is not your fault. She is *not* your responsibility, Jessica. The repercussions of her actions are not your cross to bear, no matter how much this town might want you to believe that. You are your own person.

You make your own decisions. The only behavior you have to answer for is yours. Understood?"

Jessica could hardly listen when so much of her attention was spent biting back tears and repeating, *Don't cry, stupid!* over and over again in her mind. But she instinctually recognized the body language of a request for agreement, so she nodded.

Mrs. Thomas shifted her hefty frame and stood, using Jess's shoulders as leverage. "I knew you would. You're a smart girl, Jessica. Not everyone makes it out of this town, but I know you will. You have a bright future ahead of you if you don't absorb the dead-end behaviors of the adults around you. Come on now." She motioned toward the classroom. "Let's have a good day, shall we?"

When she grinned, Jessica returned the expression on reflex then scurried into the classroom before her teacher could see the faked mirth slide away, replaced by the deep sadness and confusion brawling inside her chest, landing stray kicks and punches to her lungs.

Jess walked past Miranda and took a seat at the back of the classroom. She set down her backpack, took out her notebook, and waited for her friend to join her.

"What was that about?" Miranda whispered as she lowered herself into a seat next to Jess.

Mrs. Thomas returned to her desk like nothing had happened and settled in, marking papers while the rest of the students arrived and found their seats, forced to adapt to Jessica and Miranda's change of location.

Jess kept her eyes on her teacher, whom she suspected

wouldn't approve of the gossip, and spoke softly. "My mom beat up Mrs. Wurst yesterday after school."

When Miranda didn't immediately speak, Jessica turned to face her, sure she was about to get a second lecture.

Miranda's white-blonde eyebrows arched high above her big blue eyes and her mouth hung open.

"I know," Jessica said, "it was the wrong—"

Miranda blinked rapidly as her expression unfroze. "And you didn't call me right away?" She grinned and leaned forward conspiratorially. "I need to know everything! Now!"

That was more in line with the reaction Jess had hoped for from anyone who heard about the incident, and the outermost layers of shame peeled away. Jessica's eyes flickered to Mrs. Thomas, who was still staring intently down at papers, a red pen gripped in her fist.

Coast was clear.

Jess leaned toward her friend, filled her lungs with air, and then dove in. "My mom whooped ass. Even *God* was cheering her on …"

She'd replayed the story over and over again in her mind to commit it to memory and was thrilled for the opportunity to put it to theatric use. While sneaking occasional cautious glances at her teacher, Jessica recalled every kick, hair-grab, and punch, doing her best not to gesticulate, which would draw Mrs. Thomas's attention and make obvious the topic of conversation.

As she listed off the toppings on last night's double supreme pizza, Trent and Courtney slunk into the classroom and took their places in the seats farthest away from Miranda and her. She could've sworn she saw Trent limping slightly. Courtney definitely winced when she tried to sit. If she didn't know better, she would've said they were part of the brawl. Except she was there and knew that wasn't true.

Mrs. Thomas noticed the abnormalities too. Her gaze followed them as they shuffled their feet to desks against the far wall, where they slid into their seats. Courtney sluggishly unzipped her backpack and pulled out her binder, while Trent didn't bother with that, leaning forward and placing his head on the desk.

The look Mrs. Thomas then gave Jessica spoke volumes. It said, *See?* And further, *Violence affects more than those immediately involved.* Or maybe that was just Jessica's conscience telling her that. With an unexpected pang of guilt stabbing her in the sternum, Jess was forced to admit that maybe, just possibly, Mrs. Thomas had a point.

The Wursts sat there dejectedly, like two scolded dogs. Trent's knees bounced up and down rapidly while his forehead remained glued to the desk, and Courtney stared out the window, her hands folded neatly on her binder.

Why do I feel bad for them? They deserved it.

She'd posed the question to herself, not expecting a reply, but she got one anyway.

THEY DID.

Then why do I feel bad?

BECAUSE YOU CAN FEEL BAD FOR PEOPLE WHO GET WHAT THEY DESERVE.

A moral discrepancy nagged at her still. So she decided to tap the source of all moral discrepancies for an answer.

Was it wrong for Mom to beat up Mrs. Wurst?

There was stillness in her mind, and Jessica wondered if God had vanished on her again.

Then: *IF IT WAS WRONG, I DON'T WANT TO BE RIGHT.*

Ugh. She wished He *had* vanished.

Maybe she could feel sorry for Trent and Courtney and still kind of hate them. Maybe those emotions could exist at the same time.

Either way, she didn't have to relate to the Wurst twins in class, and with both in lunch detention for the week, she got to enjoy her food without accidentally feeling sorry for them.

During math class that afternoon, they practiced multiplying three-digit numbers. Jess found it frustratingly easy, like most math, and was forced to find ways to keep herself preoccupied once she'd finished her worksheet.

She often concocted real-life applications to keep her mind busy. Once, after watching a documentary about the reproductive process of Galapagos turtles, she calculated the number of years females must lay eggs for the population to remain consistent. She took into account the number of eggs laid, the mortality rate, and the estimated population—all numbers she'd memorized without meaning to—and chipped away at a solution while the rest of her classmates struggled with remainders.

Today, however, there was another real-world formula that ate away at her, the seed of which had been deeply planted the day before, and not even Destinee's epic (albeit *wrong*) ass whooping could root it from the soil of Jessica's subconscious.

To be fair, it wasn't a *real-life* application so much as a *theoretical-death* one.

She started by calculating the number of days until her twelfth birthday. One hundred and fifty. Then she worked out an equation.

$$(33 - 12) \times 365 = 7{,}665$$

Then she counted the leap days in the next twenty-one years and built a complete equation.

$$7{,}665 + 5 + 150 = 7{,}820$$

She sighed.

Fewer than eight thousand days left to live unless she could find a way to make herself much more likable and much less killable.

She wasn't sure which one seemed like more of an impossible task.

Chapter Twelve

12 AGC

Seven thousand four hundred and eighteen days left. Jessica scribbled it down in her notebook next to the date and her name. Twelve years old was a little soon to start worrying about death, but she took that fear and slipped it in the massive mental filing cabinet labeled "weird things in my life." She was closer to seven thousand days than she was eight thousand now, and she couldn't believe how time had snuck by.

Without realizing it, she'd almost completed her first school year at Marymoore Junior High without anything too terrible happening.

While she hadn't found ways to be less killable, she'd learned a few tricks to be more likable—laughing at other people's jokes, complimenting her cooler classmates' clothes and hair, and hiding her grades from everyone but Miranda, who had promised to be better about not blurting them out. But most of all, Jess had learned that the key to being liked was to never say anything about herself.

It'd gotten her through three-quarters of the year with minimal grief, so she intended to do it for the remaining 7,418 days of her life.

Mr. Foster, her seventh-grade science teacher, waved at the students from the front of the classroom to get their attention one last time before the end of the school day. The room was by no means quiet or focused, but he dove into his announcement anyway. "Now before you leave for the weekend, I need all of you to listen closely. Each of you must take one of these permission slips home to get your parent or guardian to sign it. You need to bring this back *signed* Monday morning. I cannot stress that enough. *You need to get this signed.* Write it on your hand if you have to, just do it."

He had their attention now. Mr. Foster was a young, clean-cut man with a nest of short blond curls on his crown that Jess always wished he would grow out. He was only a few years out of college and seemed much too tired and apathetic for someone his age. His usual announcements consisted of a monotone explanation ending with, "or whatever," so the fact that he stressed the importance of this meant it was something big. So big, in fact, that it required a parent signature.

Only one other time that year had a permission slip seemed so important, and that was when Ms. Morris wanted to show a PG-13 film about Lincoln, in social studies and compare it to primary source documents. Despite the fact that the movie was about something everyone knew would be dull, the fact that it was PG-13 had caused quite a stir among her classmates. Students became divided into two distinct social groups: those whose parents allowed them to watch PG-13 movies and those whose parents were hard-ass jerks. She hadn't been sure where she fell in the groups because she didn't watch a lot of movies. But she couldn't imagine her mother ever telling her not to watch one because she wasn't old enough.

The movie hadn't presented a problem for Jessica's social standing. When she'd handed that permission slip to her mother, Destinee had scanned it and muttered, "Damn, this sounds boring," before signing without any mention of the rating.

Destinee rarely did more than quickly scan permission slips before signing them, so whatever this one was that Mr. Foster began handing out, Jess was sure it would be no big deal.

At least Mr. Foster was their science teacher, so Jess felt confident that it wouldn't be another history movie. Social studies was always Jessica's least favorite subject, for one main reason: God loved providing commentary.

ARE YOU KIDDING ME? MENTALLY UNSTABLE? MARY TODD WAS A SAINT. YOU KNOW WHAT I HEARD ABE SAY ABOUT SLAVES ONCE? ...

It usually devolved into gossip that Jess didn't care much for. Benjamin Franklin had a thing for feet, John D. Rockefeller was able to speak backward in German and so on and so forth until Jess couldn't remember any of the important information for her tests, like dates and who killed whom.

Mr. Foster paced up and down the rows of desks, handing a slip to each student. "Seeing as how you're now in the *Battle Royale* we call junior high, your bodies are changing, et cetera, et cetera, and the state of Texas wants you to learn the bare minimum about sex so that you can feel really bad about having it and end up with lots of kids before you're ready."

When Mr. Foster placed the paper face down on her desk, Jess swiped it, flipped it over, and started reading the information.

Sex education.

Finally.

Now she might actually understand what God was talking about half the time. Chris Riley—he'd dropped the -*topher* at some point during the previous summer—raised his hand from beside her, and when Mr. Foster finished handing out the papers and looked up, he called on the boy.

"What does the word ab— ab-stin-ence mean?"

Mr. Foster leaned back on his desk and sighed heavily. "It means that you shouldn't have sex until you're married, at which point I'm sure you can easily flip the *off* switch on your lifelong shame mechanism and enjoy years of wonderful fulfilling relations with your hetero, God-fearing spouse."

Judging by the look on Chris's face, that didn't answer his question, but Mr. Foster was clearly done talking about it. "Remember, you have to turn that back in. And make sure your parents know that there's a screening of the content tomorrow night. Here. At the school. So they can approve all the material you'll be shown, in case they're still under the delusion that they can protect you from exposure to what they deem inappropriate despite buying you an iPhone this summer to use at your leisure."

Mr. Foster always talked like that. The only time he didn't seem so tired and agitated was when he was talking about science; everything else in life seemed to drain him, especially anything relating to Texas, education, administration, parents, testing, race relations, religion, and young people.

He was Jess's favorite teacher at Marymoore Junior High.

After he had written their homework for the weekend on the board, he turned to the class and dismissed them with, "Go forth and abstain!"

She slid her permission slip into her backpack and walked out of the class with Miranda, Sandra, Courtney, and a new girl named Emma who had moved from California at the start of the school year (and whose Unofficial Devil Test results were, of course, inconclusive). She was pretty, blonde (though only through the use of harsh chemicals), and immediately Sandra's best friend.

"In Cali, we had sex ed back in third grade," said Emma. "I'm sure I already know everything."

Jess had enjoyed the fascinating interplay in her new group of friends once Emma had shown up on the first day with her curled hair, golden-tan skin, blue eyes, and—most noteworthy of all—breasts. Everyone had flocked to her, and the fact that she didn't hate Jess was probably the only reason why she was allowed around now. In fact, on two occasions, Emma had actually been *nice* to Jess, once complimenting the natural highlights in her ash brown hair, and later proclaiming that she wanted to be in Jess's book group for language arts because Jess was, "the smartest girl in the class." That last one had clearly left Courtney raw, but the Wurst girl craved nothing more than Emma's approval, so no retribution had come Jessica's way because of it.

"But like, even before third grade I already knew what sex was," Emma tacked on for good measure.

"Oh yeah, me too," Courtney chimed in. "Not that I've had sex ed … Although we did have this speaker come talk to us about sex in Youth last year, but, I mean, I already knew everything before that."

Jess looked at Miranda, who rolled her eyes subtly. Good. She wasn't the only one who wasn't buying what Courtney was selling.

"Sex is so gross, though," Courtney said. "Like, sooo gross. And it's basically the biggest sin you can commit. You know who has sex outside of marriage? Animals. Reverend Dean says that if we want to be any better than gross, lowly animals, we need to not have sex until marriage."

And there it was.

Mentioning Jimmy had become Courtney's only way to take a stab at Jess without Emma catching wind of infighting. The tactic was similarly effective in their classes where Emma wasn't present because Courtney knew Mrs.

Thomas—now Assistant Principal Thomas—couldn't discipline her for simply mentioning her reverend's name.

"I dunno," Sandra said. "Sex is pretty gross, but boys aren't always gross."

The girls had congregated around Emma's locker, which was the established hub where their little clique stopped to reflect on the day after school let out.

"You know who's actually pretty cute?" Emma asked, looking like she had a real secret. Not a *HITLER ACTUALLY DIED IN 1953* secret, but a secret all the same.

"Who?" Sandra demanded.

"Chris Riley."

Immediately Jess's eyes darted to Miranda's face. Her friend wore an expertly crafted mask of passivity, but she knew Miranda was not all right with sharing her long-time crush with the new popular girl, who apparently also didn't realize that Sandra and Chris had dated all last year.

"Oh my gosh, I think so, too!" Courtney said.

"Hey wait," Miranda said, squinting at Sandra and tapping her lips with her pointer finger, pretending to recall some faint memory. "Didn't you and Chris go out most of last year?"

Emma's head jerked around toward Sandra. "Wait, really?"

Sandra shifted uncomfortably from one foot to the other, and there was a two-second delay between when she opened her mouth and when sound finally came out. "Yeah, I mean, for a little bit. But it's whatever. I'm so over him. I mean, yeah, he's cute, but I'm over him."

Jess was tempted to point out that it had been Chris

who had dumped Sandra, but she didn't feel like being a pariah, so she stayed quiet.

Emma tucked in her chin and cocked her head to the side. "Oh, well, um. I mean, I was totally going to go for him, but if you don't want me to—"

"No!" Sandra blurted. "No, I mean, yeah, it's fine if you want to go for him. That's fine. I don't even care. Like, seriously. I'm so over him."

Emma didn't need more convincing, and her concern vanished in a puff, leading Jessica to believe that it had been nothing more than an act to begin with. "Okay, cool. Yeah, that's good, because I'm pretty sure he likes me."

In a moment of impeccable timing, Chris walked by, engrossed in conversation with Trent and an eighth grader named Ben—something about football—and the girls erupted in giggles as the boys passed. Jess focused her eyes on Chris, searching for what it was the other girls and Miranda saw in him. She supposed he did have nice, silky dirty-blond hair, and he somehow managed to keep a dark tan all year round. He was also funny, and even though he wasn't particularly studious, he was always the team captain in PE and never failed to pick her first out of the girls. Granted, it was obvious from a multitude of his offhanded comments that he still considered himself under imminent threat of smiting, and on more than one occasion in the heat of play he'd jokingly referred to her as his lucky charm, so maybe that had more to do with it than him being nice or her having any athletic talent.

But it didn't matter because once she actually added up

all those little things about Christopher Riley, they amounted to one clear reality.

Oh no. I think I have a crush on Chris now.

She tried not to let the panic show on her face, but she failed, because when Chris, all confidence and smiles, looked over at the giggling girls and his eyes met hers, the glow of his face darkened instantly and his grin drooped at the corners as his eyes popped open in shock and ... fear? Crap! She hadn't meant to spook him by staring at him like that; she was just confused. He hurried on past her group of friends and glanced back at her over his shoulder one last time before disappearing out of sight around the corner.

"Oh my gosh," Sandra said. "I think he's scared of Jessica."

Jess looked around at her friends and felt her face flush.

"I don't blame him," Courtney said. "We all know she's a little crazy."

When Emma and Sandra started to giggle, Jess forced out a laugh too. Because laughing was all she *could* do if she wanted to keep the precarious friendships she'd scrounged together. It was a minor sacrifice when it came down to it. And this wasn't elementary school anymore; this was junior high. Being popular was a zero-sum game, one her life literally depended on if she ever wanted to see thirty-four.

Chapter Thirteen

Jess hadn't expected it to be so difficult to ask her mom to sign the permission slip. It was just a stupid piece of paper. But the walk home from school had allowed her time to consider the ramifications of broaching the subject of sex with her mother, and, though she didn't know much about it, she knew the basics. As with religion, most of her knowledge on the subject had been absorbed through social osmosis.

She was aware that sex involved being naked with someone else. She also knew basically all animals had sex, and that for humans, at least, there were multiple sex positions and "giraffe" was one. And babies could result from it.

Those were the facts as she understood them. When it came to opinions, however, the world seemed a bit conflicted. Everyone at school acted like sex was a big deal (even if Emma acted blasé about it), but Destinee seemed to believe the opposite.

It wasn't a common topic around the McCloud home, but when it came up, it was never in the hushed tones everyone else used. In fact, it was usually talked of quite loudly.

Jessica suspected that presenting the permission slip would invite unwanted discussion. Obviously, she was curious, but she'd worked hard to build an invisible barrier between her mother and herself over the past year when it came to anything personal (sex seeming the most personal of all topics since it involved the private parts). A piece of paper with the word "sex" on it multiple times might be just the sledgehammer Destinee needed to break down that wall. And who knew what kind of personal stories would follow.

But Mr. Foster had been clear about getting it signed, and Jess definitely didn't want to be the only one who had to sit out during sex ed.

So, once she threw her bag down by the kitchen table and Destinee walked in from whatever she was doing in the bedroom, Jess worked up the courage she needed by reminding herself how it would feel to have to miss out on what all her friends would undoubtedly spend the last week before spring break discussing.

She pulled the permission slip from her backpack. "So, like, Mr. Foster said we need our parents to sign this ... or whatever," she finished, taking a page from Mr. Foster's book of How to Not Give a Shit.

"Uh, okay." Destinee looked for a pen, found one in their crap drawer, and walked over to the table, where she leaned over, holding the form down with her left hand and hastily scanning for where to sign. Once she found it, she lowered the pen to the paper, and for a split second, Jess thought that maybe her mom wouldn't read it and all the worrying had been for nothing.

She let herself relax and sat down across the table from where her mother stood.

But then Destinee laughed. "Oh shit. They got y'all doing this in the seventh grade? You poor things. Don't eat anything before watching the slideshow."

"What slideshow?"

Destinee continued reading the handout and the amusement disappeared from her face.

"What slideshow?" Jess asked, desperate for an answer.

"Son of a bitch."

"What? What is it?"

Destinee rotated the permission slip so it was right-side-up for Jess and pointed to a section at the bottom. "You didn't even read this, did you?"

"No, why?" Jess leaned in to see. In tiny letters at the bottom of the page was, *A White Light Ministries Community Service.*

"Jesus," said Destinee. "This is going to be a goddamn mess. I have half a mind to check *No* on this thing and educate you on sex myself."

"Please don't."

Destinee eyed her daughter closely. "Yeah, I guess I don't know much about it either, outside of how to do it and how to get knocked up. That's likely more than you'll learn from these uptight folks, though, so don't be expecting anything useful. You're probably better off just watching a few more of those nature shows."

Jess took a deep breath and let it out slowly when Destinee finally checked the *Yes* box and signed the paper. "I don't want you to be one of those kids who grows up ashamed of sex, but I also don't want you to be one of the kids who gets made fun of for not getting to do the sex ed. So just do me a favor and don't listen to anything they tell you, and then you and I will learn about good sex together ... in like, five years. Does that work?"

Jess nodded and wanted nothing more than for this conversation to end.

"But you gotta promise me one thing, Jess. You gotta promise you won't have sex before we get a chance to learn about good sex, okay?"

"Okay." That was an easy enough promise to make, considering Jess had no desire to ever have sex with anyone, based upon the little she knew about it.

Destinee looked down at the paper again. "Abstinence. Ha! Do you know what abstinence is?"

Jess tried to remember Mr. Foster's explanation, but it was too complicated. "No."

"It means not having sex till you're married."

"Why would people wait until marriage?"

Destinee thought about that for a second. "Because it's the right thing to do, I guess."

"So ... are you and God married?"

"No."

"Were God and Jesus's mom—"

"Mary," supplied Destinee.

"Were God and Mary married?"

Destinee squinted at the air above Jess's left shoulder and pursed her lips slightly. "I don't *think* so."

"But if waiting till marriage is the right thing to do, then why didn't God do it?"

Destinee sighed and sat down in a chair across from Jess. "Well, I guess because it's not a practical thing to do. And he's God. He makes the rules, so he can be the exception to the rule."

That sounded like God logic.

"Five years, though, baby. You gotta wait five years."

Till she was seventeen? Yeah, no problem there. That was how old her mother was when she'd had her, though. A brand-new question surfaced in Jess's mind, and because she was thinking in terms of math, it slipped from her lips before she could stop it. "Wait, how old were you when you first had sex?"

Destinee jumped up from the table. "You hungry? I was thinking spaghetti tonight."

Chapter Fourteen

"I basically know all there is to know about sex," Chris said as Jess approached the small group standing just outside her homeroom the following Thursday morning. Miranda was looking at him with a pained expression, as was Trent. "How do you know everything already?" Trent asked.

Chris opened his mouth to reply but then noticed Jessica. "Uhh ... I don't know. We should get to class."

She glared at him. "You don't have to stop talking just because I'm here."

"Uh, yeah I do."

Jessica shook her head slightly. "Why? I'm not going to be offended."

"Because you're the daughter of God." The words tumbled out of his mouth like he was vomiting them.

"No, she's not," Trent began. But then he seemed to remember something, and he glanced at Jess and swallowed down the rest of what he was planning to say.

"Yes, she is, Trent," Miranda said loyally.

"It doesn't matter either way," Jess interjected. "It's not like I'm a spy for him. He can hear what you say and see what you do no matter where I am. And trust me, he doesn't care." As a last-ditch effort, she added, "Also, have you met my mom?"

But Chris wasn't buying it. "We better get to class."

How did people not understand how God worked? She wasn't going to tattle on anyone, because that was entirely unnecessary. God already knew, and for the most part, He didn't seem to care much. About anything.

The throng of students in the hallway parted for Mrs. Thomas, who shooed away the boys to Mr. Foster's and Mr. Miller's classrooms, where they would be educated on sex separately from the girls. Jess was glad about that. Almost more so than she was about it being the last day before spring break.

All thirty-two of the sixth-grade girls were rounded up into one of the larger classrooms, meaning Jess had no chance of being allowed a respite from the company of Courtney, Emma, and Sandra, which she really could have used, despite them now being her friends.

The desks had been removed from the room to accommodate more chairs, and as Jess filed in with her clique, she saw Mrs. Thomas standing at the front with two women Jess didn't recognize, not even a little bit. One was tall and fit, with long, straightened chestnut hair and a heart-shaped face. Jess couldn't guess the woman's age. From the way she stood and the way she dressed—sharp, professional, with a bright blue satin shirt under a chocolate brown suit jacket and matching pants—Jess guessed her to be in her late thirties. But her face was sweet and youthful, with freckles spattered over the bridge of her small but sharp nose and a complete lack of bags under her eyes. Jess wanted to like this woman.

The second woman was even shorter and rounder than Mrs. Thomas, easily pushing two-fifty, with thick, coarse black hair that she slicked back into a tight braid and might have served well as a helmet, considering the amount of gel holding it in place. Her smile appeared surgically pinned to her face and clashed with the intensity in her eyes as she scanned each of the girls from head to toe as they passed. When Emma passed in her short-shorts, the woman's gaze lingered on the girl's thighs and her smile melted into a disapproving frown while her eyes narrowed.

Mrs. Thomas waited for the students to be seated but not for the anxious chatter to die down before she addressed the class. "You all know me," she said, and the chatter ceased immediately, "and I hope that you feel comfortable enough to talk about sex in front of me. Much to Sandra's chagrin, I'm sure, I have an active sex life in my marriage"—all eyes turned to Sandra, whose face instantly drained of color before her cheeks glowed bright red—"and I don't want you to be scared to ask your questions about sex. Now's the time because we have with us today Dr. Monica Fractal"—at the mention of the name, Emma leaned over and whispered excitedly to Sandra, though Jess wasn't sure why—"and Mrs. Jamie Reyes. Doctor Fractal is a gynecologist over at Midland Memorial Hospital, and Mrs. Reyes is part of the sex education program that our school leaders and PTA have contracted out to." Mrs. Thomas smiled stiffly, her lips peeling back to bare her teeth while the skin around her eyes remained unmoved. "Now. Before we start, does anyone have any questions for Dr. Fractal or Mrs. Reyes?"

Emma's hand shot up and Mrs. Thomas pointed to her. "Are you related to Jameson Fractal?"

The majority of the class giggled. Jess had zero idea why.

Dr. Fractal smiled. "Yes. He's my little brother."

As most of the girls gasped and some idiot screamed, Jess leaned over to Miranda to whisper, "Who's that?"

Miranda leaned back, turned to Jess, and shrugged.

Mrs. Thomas quieted down the class. "Okay, now that we have that out of the way, do we have any *sex education* questions right off the bat?"

The class was still lost in a torrent of whispers though, and no one seemed to have education—not even pertaining to sex—on the mind.

"Okay, then. We'll go ahead and get started." She headed to her laptop as Mrs. Reyes and Dr. Fractal took a seat in two chairs at the front of the classroom, facing the whiteboard that displayed the projection. "We're going to get started by watching a short video that will teach us about the female body." Mrs. Thomas pressed play, and as the movie began, she took her seat next to Dr. Fractal.

The background music was flat and wobbly, and the drawings reminded Jess of the *Looney Tunes* she sometimes watched when nature shows either weren't on or were about boring things like human tribes.

"You may feel some changes in your body that seem scary—but don't worry! They're completely normal and just as God intended."

Jess could feel eyes dart to her face at the mention of God. But she kept her gaze focused on the projection and tried to ignore it, which was easy enough to do when her mind was busy scrambling to make sense of the information being presented in the form of bolded captions and poorly animated images.

Oh, and then there was the *blood*. How had no one mentioned the blood before? Sure, she knew that female mammals went into heat, but she'd always assumed humans were the exception, because if they weren't, it seemed like *someone* would have mentioned it to her, even if it was as simple as, "Oh, by the way, enjoy life while you can, because at some point soon you'll start bleeding from your vagina for one week out of every month." The fact that men didn't have to deal with anything even close to that—at least that she knew about yet—seemed grossly unfair. How was she supposed to get anything done during the week she was bleeding? It was like someone was stealing a quarter of her adult life from her and saying, "See? Women are doomed from the start."

God. He did this. This had His fingerprints all over it. As soon as she was done taking in all the ammunition she could get from this video, He would be hearing from her.

The video ended on a graphic of clouds floating in a serene blue sky before parting to make way for the important takeaways, which were written in bold, red letters that floated closer to the viewer, where they hovered until the narrator could read through each of them.

- *The female body is full of mystery and awe*
- *Your body is a temple that should not be tainted until marriage*
- *Menstruation is the body's way of cleansing itself once a month*
- *Tampons and contraceptives can cause cervical cancer and unsightly stretching that will make sex less pleasurable for your future husband*

The video ended and the image changed to the desktop of Mrs. Thomas's laptop, a picture of a fiery orange sun setting over a field of bluebonnets. The room was silent as Mrs. Thomas stood, cleared her throat, and walked over to cue up the next video without saying a word.

God! GOD!

Jess waited for an answer. When she didn't receive one she tried to think of ways to force Him to show up. Persistence was the only thing she could think of.

God! Where are you? I need to talk to you! Now! God!

SO DEMANDING. WHAT DO YOU WANT?

Where did she even start?

Why do girls have to have periods but boys don't?

OH ME. MUST WE HAVE THIS TALK RIGHT NOW?

Obviously not, because you make the rules, but come on! What's with menstruation?

PLEASE. IT'S REALLY NOT THAT BAD.

You have a lot of nerve to make women deal with that and then say it's really not that bad.

TOUCHE, BUT AT LEAST YOU HAVE TAMPONS FOR IT

NOW. AND MEDICATION. BOTH ARE MIRACULOUS, AND TRUST ME, I WOULD KNOW.

But tampons cause cancer and unsightly stretching.

SAYS WHO?

You, I thought.

NOPE. WASN'T ME.

Okay, then this video said it.

OH. UM. NO, I DON'T THINK THAT'S CORRECT.

You're not sure how the female body works?!

LISTEN, I'VE BEEN SORT OF HANDS OFF WITH ALL THAT SINCE ORIGINAL MISTAKE. I LET EVOLUTION RUN ITS COURSE.

Ugh. You're no help.

Mrs. Thomas introduced the next video. "This one is about how boys' bodies work so that you're not completely taken by surprise when they start acting weird around you."

This video seemed about as old as the first, but instead of the background music being mostly flutes and some piano, the video faded in from black to the sound of gunfire and war drums.

"Men … the sex that stands between safety and chaos. The protectors of the innocent and bringers of justice …"

Jess accidentally zoned out until a giant cartoon of a penis appeared on the whiteboard. She didn't have to know about sex to recognize a penis when she saw one. All animals had them.

"When a man becomes sexually aroused, blood pumps into the penis to prepare him for intercourse, if necessary. For a young man, anything from the picture of a naked woman to a girl wearing a

knee-length skirt can set off arousal, making it difficult for him to complete whatever task is at hand, even if it's something as important as defending this great nation from Communists or Orientals ..."

THEY REALLY NEED A NEW VIDEO.

What are Orientals?

ASIANS.

Wait. Like Stephanie Lee? Why do we need to be defended from them?

YOU DON'T.

I'm confused.

THAT'S OKAY.

This video finished up with similar bullet points as the first, though the tone of the narrator's voice was markedly more assertive.

- *Erections can be triggered by any female*
- *A male with an erection will find it difficult to make good choices*
- *Females in provocative clothing risk being raped*
- *Keeping women out of the military is a necessary step for national security*

By the time the video ended, Dr. Fractal was visibly upset, with stress lines cutting across her forehead, tipping the balance and pushing her appearance closer to forty than twenty. But Mrs. Reyes's eyes finally matched her plastered grin as she sat up straight in her chair, her hands folded in her lap.

"Okay," Mrs. Thomas continued, sounding exhausted.

"*One* more video. I think this one needs no introduction, even if I *could* find the proper words to give it context."

She pressed play, and returned in her chair to face the projection wall.

The image of a dried up desert hellscape faded in from black and suddenly the word *AIDS* appeared on the screen, each letter drawn to look like it was covered in cracked skin.

A gruff male voice began the narration. *"By the time you know you have it, it's already too late."* There was the sound of a man screaming in agony followed by a heart rate monitor beeping slowly and steadily. *"It is a death sentence passed from one person to another through impure sex."* The heart rate monitor flatlined. *"There is only one way to make sure you do not contract it, and that is abstinence."*

UNLESS YOU'RE A DRUG USER SHARING NEEDLES OR SOMEONE WITH HIV RAPES YOU, OR YOUR OPEN WOUND PRESSES UP AGAINST THE OPEN WOUND OF SOMEONE INFECTED, OR, REALLY, I COULD JUST GIVE IT TO PEOPLE. I'VE DONE IT BEFORE, AND I'D DO IT AGAIN.

God droned on for most of the video, and by the end Jess felt like AIDS was probably an inevitable part of life. There were so many ways to get it, it seemed, despite the checklist of takeaways at the end:

- *AIDS originated from human-monkey intercourse*
- *AIDS is spread through homosexual intercourse*
- *AIDS is a death sentence*
- *The two most affected communities are homosexuals and Africans*

"Okay!" Mrs. Thomas flipped on the light switch and turned to the class. "Any questions about AIDS?"

Courtney raised her hand and was called on. "Why are there so many homosexuals in Africa?"

Mrs. Thomas deflated and pinched the bridge of her nose. "Dr. Fractal? You want this one?"

"Definitely." The doctor stood up and cleared her throat. "To answer your question, Courtney, I can see where that video might have led you to believe, based on the tragically flawed information it presented, that if AIDS is the disease of the gay community, and so many in Africa have it, that Africa must have a large gay community. That is not in fact accurate. The part about Africa having an AIDS epidemic is true, but not the part about AIDS being mostly contained within the gay community."

"Actually ..." Mrs. Reyes stood and faced the class. "Let me clarify what the doctor is saying here." She smiled at Dr. Fractal, who appeared too stunned to continue. "There's a push by the leftist media to say that just about *anyone* could get AIDS, as if you could get it simply from standing too close to a gay man at a grocery store." She chuckled. "But thank God that's not true. People who have AIDS have either had sex with a man who chose to be gay or had sex with someone who had sex with a man who chose to be gay. Does that answer your question?"

Courtney shook her head. "No."

Emma raised her arm up into the air and Mrs. Thomas sighed and pointed to her.

"I have an uncle back in SoCal who's gay. Does that

mean my uncle has AIDS, and if I shared a drink with him, could I have it too?"

Mrs. Reyes looked like she was about to speak, but Dr. Fractal beat her to it. "No. Absolutely not. Not every gay man has AIDS or HIV. And I don't know your history, but there is very little chance, statistically speaking, that you have AIDS. But if you are still concerned, ask your doctor about it."

"How about this," Mrs. Reyes began. "Raise your hand if you've ever had sex."

"No!" Mrs. Thomas interjected, stepping forward quickly. She turned to the class. "No one raise your hand!" She rounded on Mrs. Reyes. "Jamie, you can't just ask that."

Mrs. Reyes shrugged. "Doesn't matter if I know or not. God knows either way. He knows what each and every person does behind closed doors."

IT'S TRUE. SHE HASN'T HAD SEX WITH HER HUSBAND IN SIX YEARS AND THREE MONTHS.

"I hate to even ask," said Mrs. Thomas, "but any other questions?"

No one raised a hand. "Good. I mean, not 'good,' but 'okay.' So what we're going to do is hand out these slips of paper, and you'll write down any questions you might want to ask anonymously, meaning you don't write your name on them and no one needs to know it was you who asked. Then we'll mix them all up, and Dr. Fractal will go through and answer them."

"And Mrs. Reyes," said Mrs. Reyes.

Without missing a beat, Mrs. Thomas replied, "Actually, I think it would be best if we got a doctor's perspective."

The skin around Mrs. Reyes's lips tightened, and she inhaled deeply, puffing up and lifting her chin high. "The school hired *me* to oversee this because they didn't want to give a secular doctor free rein to poison the minds of our daughters—"

"I'm a Methodist," Dr. Fractal said flatly. "Not that it actually matters."

Mrs. Reyes folded her arms across her chest. "Methodist! Hmph! Sounds about right."

Dr. Fractal did a good job of containing the anger Jess could feel radiating off of her in waves.

Once Mrs. Thomas had finished handing out slips of paper, each girl got to work writing down her questions. Jess had a difficult time thinking of a good one, but ultimately settled on *Are there ways to stop having your period?*

She folded the piece of paper in half and slipped it into the glass fishbowl Mrs. Thomas brought by on her way back up to the front of the room. Dr. Fractal reached inside the bowl and selected a question. Her eyes skimmed over it, then she sighed and her shoulders sagged before she read it aloud. "The question is, *What is sex?*"

She looked sympathetically out onto her audience. "I feel like this is a realistic question, considering the information you've been provided. Sex, or the act of vaginal sex, is when the man's penis becomes erect from arousal and penetrates—"

"That's enough," said Mrs. Reyes curtly from beside the doctor. "That's *quite* enough."

"What do you mean? I was just explaining sex in sex education ..."

"Yes." Mrs. Reyes scoffed and looked uncomfortable. "Yes, you were. This is not *pornography* education, Dr. Fractal."

"I don't believe I was being pornographic. They've already learned about erections and vaginas. I'm just explaining the interaction between the two."

Mrs. Reyes scoffed. "I *know* that's what you were doing, and using superfluous, titillating language, no less—"

"That's inaccurate. I was using scientific terminology ..."

IT'S WHEN A PENIS GOES INSIDE A VAGINA, JUST SO YOU KNOW.

I got that. It wasn't my question.

YOU SHOULD LET YOUR CLASS KNOW.

Uh, no.

SORRY, LET ME REPHRASE. THOU SHALT LET THE CLASS KNOW.

I hate you.

"Hey, it's when a penis goes inside a vagina," Jessica blurted. The adults in the room jerked around to face her. Mrs. Thomas was smiling, Dr. Fractal was trying not to smile, and Mrs. Reyes's mouth hung open in horror.

She managed to peel her eyes away from the women to turn in her seat and look at the rest of her female classmates, for whom the factual statement was actually intended.

They were stunned silent, but whether that was because of the content or because she wasn't known for outbursts like this, which seemed brazen given the context, was unclear. Courtney must have believed whatever came next for Jessica would be unpleasant, because the girl's wide eyes shined like someone had just presented her with a glittery new gift. Otherwise, the faces around the room appeared in various states of pain and anguish, eyes darting from Jessica to the women at the front. The anticipation over what happened next was palpable.

Miranda, however, smiled proudly at Jessica.

But Jess wasn't proud of herself. Nor was she smiling.

I hate you so much for this.

THEY NEEDED TO KNOW.

So now I'm your puppet? I have to say whatever you tell me to?

WITH HOW OFTEN YOU SAY THE WRONG THING, THE GOOD LORD FIGURED YOU MIGHT APPRECIATE THE HELP HERE AND THERE.

Giggling erupted around the room almost simultaneously. The shock had thinned, replaced by the reality of Jessica having said "penis" and "vagina" in the same sentence.

"Can you believe her?" Mrs. Reyes said to Mrs. Thomas. "Are you going to just let her spew that kind of filth?"

Mrs. Thomas stared Mrs. Reyes in the eyes. "Yes."

Mrs. Reyes huffed a bit, then returned to her seat, grabbed her phone from her purse, and began texting excitedly.

"Next question!" said Dr. Fractal, more energetically. She opened another slip of paper and immediately began reading it aloud. *"What is … Oh, that's the same question. Um …* Yeah, so it's when a man puts his penis in a woman's vagina. Essentially. There's a little more to it, but we'll start with that." Her eyes darted over toward Mrs. Reyes, who was still angrily texting and shaking her head.

Dr. Fractal shrugged it off, unfolded another question —"Same question. Okay ..."—went through a few more slips, and then finally got to a different one. "Ah, here we are. How does pregnancy happen?" She nodded approvingly. "This is a good one to know. During sex, the male's penis is stimulated from the friction of the movement in and out of the woman's vagina—"

"Pornography!" Mrs. Reyes exclaimed from her chair without bothering to look up from her phone.

"Anyway. After enough stimulation, the male will ejaculate and semen will be released from his penis and flow into the woman's vaginal canal and ..."

Jess continued to listen to Dr. Fractal with rapt interest. There was something entrancing about the woman's voice when describing science. She would make a good narrator for a nature show. Maybe not David Attenborough good, but good enough that Jess could imagine listening to her talk about arctic foxes or bottlenose dolphins for a couple hours, no problem.

"Does a baby happen every time?" Miranda asked from beside her.

"There are many ways to avoid pregnancy, but if you don't practice any of them, there is a good chance that not only will you become pregnant, but you've put yourself at risk of contracting an infection or disease."

"Like AIDS?" asked Stephanie from a few rows over.

Dr. Fractal conceded with a nod. "Yeah, that's entirely

possible. But more likely you'll contract a treatable infection like—"

"Okay!" Mrs. Reyes set her phone down on the chair and popped up. "I hope you've gotten your fill of pornography, because I'm now finished reporting this pervert to the White Light Sex Education Committee, and I'll take it from here." She reached into the bowl and pulled out a slip of paper, reading it, shaking her head disapprovingly, and tossing it into the discard pile before drawing another. "Ah, this one is good. It says, *Are there other diseases I can get from sex?* The answer is *absolutely*. There are more diseases that can be passed through sex than *can't* be passed through sex."

Dr. Fractal positioned herself behind Mrs. Reyes so that she could shake her head at the class and mouth, *Not true*, without the other woman noticing.

"And I actually have a slideshow of this very thing, which we were going to get to in a bit, but I think now's a good time as well."

Something tugged at Jessica's memory. Then she remembered. Her mother had mentioned the slideshow. She tried to think of what she'd eaten for breakfast and whether it might be digested by now, and as she did, the slideshow began. Each image lasted only about three seconds and included a close-up of first a vagina then a penis and testicles with the corresponding disease listed in captions at the bottom of the frame.

Girls started screaming and retching as the bumps and discoloration on each genital grew steadily more alarming.

"All these people had sex before marriage," Mrs. Reyes

proclaimed. "All of them said, 'What harm could it do? It's just the tip. God will forgive me.' And all of them were wrong."

MAKE IT STOP!

No, you *make it stop! You're God!*

RIGHT.

The images disappeared from the screen, replaced by an error message apologizing for PowerPoint's sudden failure.

The class expressed its relief through groans and cheers, with Courtney even shouting, "Praise Jesus!" Jess wanted to tell her that it was not actually Jesus but God who deserved the praise and that the two were distinct entities, but she didn't feel like starting an argument when everyone was suddenly feeling so united under one banner of nausea.

Mrs. Reyes scurried toward Mrs. Thomas's laptop and tried to solve the technical issues, but Mrs. Thomas blocked her out. "It does that sometimes. It won't work again until tomorrow, I'm afraid." She slammed the laptop shut and the projection on the whiteboard turned to solid blue.

Courtney raised her hand and Dr. Fractal pointed to her.

"What happens if you do wait until marriage and then the person you marry has a disease? How do you keep from getting it?"

Mrs. Reyes intercepted the question but gazed at Courtney sweetly. "That's why you need to make sure you marry a good man. A good man will not have slept around with the necessary prostitutes or—God forbid—gay men needed to contract one of these diseases. If he's pure of heart and body like you, there's no need to worry." She smiled reassuringly.

Dr. Fractal inserted herself between Mrs. Reyes and the class. "Or you could just get tested together. It's not the most romantic thing, but it's responsible. Most of the horrific things you saw on the slideshow are actually curable or at least treatable. And then there's always condoms."

"Whoa!" Mrs. Reyes smacked Dr. Fractal on the arm, and Jess worried the doctor might hit her back. "Stop right there. This is *abstinence* sex education, not Promiscuity 101. Plus, everyone knows that those sin balloons are more likely to break, resulting in pregnancy, than they are to *not* break."

The blood drained from Dr. Fractal's face. "That's unequivocally false."

Jess was pretty sure there was about to be a fight. If Dr. Fractal had been Destinee, there would have already been one.

YOU HAVE THE POWER TO STOP THIS, YOU KNOW.

Are you kidding me? No, I don't.

YOU'RE MY DAUGHTER. THEY'LL LISTEN TO YOU.

What do I say? I don't know anything about sex.

TELL THEM THE TRUTH. REMIND THEM YOU'RE THE DAUGHTER OF GOD AND THAT I DON'T REALLY CARE THAT MUCH IF THEY HAVE SEX BEFORE MARRIAGE, AS LONG AS IT'S CONSENSUAL AND RESPECTFUL AND THERE ARE NO NON-HUMAN ANIMALS INVOLVED.

They'll never believe me.

THAT DOESN'T MAKE IT LESS TRUE.

Please don't make me say it.

For a moment she thought He'd disappeared again.

THOU SHALT SAY IT.

Dammit.

Jess sighed heavily. She was walking into a trap, but knowing that didn't mean she could stop it without grave consequences. She hadn't listened when God thou-shalted her about Randy, and that resulted in a death by lion. Who knew what God would do to the people around her if she defied another "thou shalt" order?

She clenched her fingers into fists and then spoke loud enough to be heard over Dr. Fractal and Mrs. Reyes as God mercifully fed her the words.

"God says sex that lacks respect and consent, no matter within or without the bonds of marriage, is bad. But respectful, consensual sex, whether within or without the bonds of marriage, is not something to get all worked up about."

She paused. *Please don't make me say that.*

SAY IT.

"What we should *really* be concerning ourselves with is earthquakes in Asia. They're out of control lately. Why is no one west of the Urals talking about this?"

The room was dead silent by the time she finished, and she kept her eyes focused on the blue projection to avoid looking at any one person.

YOU DID WELL.

Let me repeat. I hate you.

Mrs. Reyes was the first to break the silence. "Well,

there you have it. The False Prophet, the daughter of a single mother, the product of promiscuity has spoken."

"I am not a false prophet." Jess dug her fingernails into her palms to brace herself against the wrath that flooded into her vicariously from God. She wanted to add *And my mother was not promiscuous,* but she figured she should pick her battles.

"Oh really?" Mrs. Reyes said. "That's interesting because a *real* prophet said you were a false one."

Wait. There was a prophet running around somewhere? "Who are you talking about?" Then it dawned on her. "Not *Jimmy*."

"Absolutely. And it shows what kind of person you are that you'd presume to be on a first-name basis with him. It's *Reverend Dean*."

"All right." Mrs. Thomas stood from her desk. "Enough of you." She walked past Mrs. Reyes and grabbed the woman's purse from beside her chair, carrying it over to the classroom door, which she opened. She turned to stare expectantly at Mrs. Reyes. When the woman didn't react, Mrs. Thomas added, "Is it just sex you don't understand, or are *hints* a mystery to you, too?"

It finally seemed to click, and Mrs. Reyes sucked in air sharply but said nothing as she headed toward the door. Then, before she shut it behind her, she turned to Mrs. Thomas one last time. "You'll be hearing about this, I assure you. Principal Mallard is a devout member of the church." Then her eyes landed on Courtney and she added, "And I'll be informing your mother about the smut they're teaching you in school. If you had any desire to remain pure, you'd follow me out this door, child."

Jess turned to look at Courtney, who was wide-eyed and terrified. She almost felt for her. It was obvious the Wurst girl was caught between getting an earful from her mother and ruining her social standing with Emma, Sandra, and the rest. But social standing won out almost immediately, and when Courtney didn't stand and grab her backpack, Mrs. Reyes huffed and harrumphed, and then turned, nose in the air, and strutted out of the room.

Mrs. Thomas shut the door remorselessly before turning back to the class. "Okay. So where were we? More questions. Dr. Fractal? Will you do us the pleasure?"

"Oh I wouldn't dare," Dr. Fractal replied, feigning scandal. "This is sex we're talking about, not pleasure. This is not pornography class."

Mrs. Thomas actually cackled at that, an uncharacteristic sound that Jess couldn't remember hearing from her before. "Okay. Next question." And the doctor reached into the fishbowl again.

With the new staffing arrangement, the experience became drastically more informative and less uncomfortable. Mrs. Thomas passed out another round of paper slips for any follow-up questions, and Jess finally began to understand how sex worked and how she could keep it from ruining her life.

The concept was still pretty gross, but it wasn't *that* gross. It was difficult for her to focus on it too much, though, with the new accusations running figure eights inside her head ...

Jimmy now called himself a prophet? That seemed a little over the top. And since when did he decide he was one? Even more confusing was the reminder that while Courtney ran with Jessica's group of friends, and might even make her top-ten list of "friends"—thanks to the small population of Mooretown—Courtney nonetheless believed that Jess was a false prophet and was therefore going to Hell. Why did that bother her so much? *Jess* knew she wasn't going to Hell. She was the daughter of God. She didn't know much about the Bible, but she was pretty sure God would never cast any of those closest to Him down into the pit of fire …

By the time Dr. Fractal had cleared up the misunderstanding of how many holes women actually had down south and what each of them were for, the morning was over.

Jess wasn't sure why the free-for-all that was lunch was the place where girls and boys were supposed to mix for the first time after learning about their bodies. It seemed entirely ill-advised.

The girls poured out into the hallway on their way to lunch, chatting and reflecting on all the information and drama of the past few hours. Jess hung a few steps back from her normal group of friends, deciding that it might be prudent to lay low for a while after speaking publicly on God's behalf. Miranda, of course, hung back with her.

Where the seventh-grade hall intersected with the main hallway, the flow of girls intermixed with the flow of boys, resulting in an uproar of giggles from the girls and uncharacteristic silence from the boys. While Jess had undoubtedly been subjected to more disturbing images in the past three hours than she had in her entire life leading up to today, the gait of the boys as they stumbled speechlessly through the halls indicated a whole other level of trauma. What on earth could have gone on in their classroom to leave them in such a state?

Jess spotted Mr. Foster as he passed by, his jaw clenched, shaking his head slowly and mumbling, "I swear to God ..." before her eyes landed on Chris Riley. The boy's usual confident posture and oblivion-based friendliness were notably absent. His shoulders slumped, and the only conclusion she could draw was that the boys had simply been chastised all morning.

"Hey, Chris," Emma said smoothly as she approached him.

He looked up and for a moment seemed awkward, but then his gaze flickered for a half second from her face to the region just below her neck, and a small smile turned the corners of his mouth. "Hey, Emma." He nodded slightly. Then his eyes wandered casually over to Jess, and the confidence disappeared instantly, replaced again by the downtroddenness of seconds before. He looked away as soon as he could.

What the heck? Did Chris assume she wouldn't approve of his flirting? Like she was Mrs. Reyes or something? Why did everyone always treat her like a killjoy?

Frustration crept up her neck and into her cheeks, growing, expanding ...

Crap, crap, crap!

Blam! A fluorescent light and its covering exploded

above Chris's head, raining shards of plastic and glass down onto him and the other students nearby. The boys and girls closest to the source of the bang yelped and fled, causing an outward stampede in all directions. Miranda flung an arm in front of Jessica, moving them both against the lockers and out of the way of the crowds.

But Chris remained planted in place. His head jerked toward Jess immediately, the fear in his eyes intensifying. It was an accusation. He was accusing her of having smote the light.

Granted, she had. She hadn't meant to, just like with the grackle, but her frustration had snuck up on her before she could contain it. And with him staring at her like that, she felt like smiting a lot more than just light bulbs. She knew better.

Jessica and Miranda were the only two of their small group remaining by the lockers after the others fled with the masses, and as Stephanie Lee elbowed past, screaming, "It's happening! Oh my God, it's happening!" Jessica figured it was time for her to get gone as well.

She flashed Miranda an apologetic grin, hoped it would suffice. She needed to find an escape route out of the building. Maybe she could make it home before anyone noticed. But when she turned, she ran straight into Mrs. Thomas.

"Why don't you follow me." It wasn't a question. The assistant principal grabbed Jess's arm and led her to the side of the hallway so that they could make their way back toward the classroom against the flow of cafeteria-bound melodrama. They stepped inside the open doorway and

Mrs. Thomas gave Jess a good long stare before speaking. "I know that was you."

"Huh?"

Was Mrs. Thomas blaming her for the unintentional and minor smiting? Obviously, it *was* Jessica's fault, but did Mrs. Thomas know that? Did her teacher believe she could do such a thing, that she possessed such a power? The woman had never expressed such beliefs, even after the grackle had rained blood and viscera on Jessica's classmates. If Mrs. Thomas meant what Jessica thought she did, this was crossing into uncharted territory.

"I know that you made that light bulb explode."

"Wait, you think I did that? I mean, I did. But you know I can smite? You actually believe I'm God's daughter?"

Mrs. Thomas nodded slowly and shut her eyes softly in a way that suggested Jess take it down a notch. "Yes, I believe you. Though I wish you'd start thinking of yourself in terms other than whose daughter you are, Jess."

It felt like a light turned on inside her chest. Mrs. Thomas believed her! She'd never doubted that Mrs. Thomas believed *in* her, but that wasn't the same as believing her father was God Himself. She'd never known how much the discrepancy had bothered her until the obstacle was finally removed, plucked from between them so that full honesty could flow, leaving no topic of Jessica's life off limits. "I hate it. I hate being God's daughter. It just gets me bullied. The only special power I have is smiting, and that gets me in trouble." She considered mentioning how being the daughter of God had also gotten Randy killed, but thought better of it. (Okay, so maybe there were still a few topics that were off limits). Considering Mrs. Thomas had been the first person to tell Jess that Randy's death wasn't her fault, admitting any guilt for the event didn't seem great for self-preservation. Or for the spectacular moment they were currently sharing. Best to tuck that memory away again. Deep, deep down.

"But don't you like being closer to ... you know, *Him?*" Mrs. Thomas's eyes lifted to the ceiling and she smiled.

"No! I can *hear* him. Not all the time, but whenever he feels like it. And it's awful! I don't even like him that much. And he never pays child support to my mom."

Mrs. Thomas chuckled, and Jess realized how much she'd just spilled to her assistant principal. No one besides Destinee, Miranda, and Jimmy knew that Jess talked directly with God on a regular basis.

She tried to gauge if God was listening in on the conversation, but she couldn't tell, and it didn't matter anyway; surely He already had a pretty good idea of her feelings about Him.

Mrs. Thomas placed a comforting hand on Jessica's shoulder. "I can see why that would be frustrating. But you can be whomever you want to be. I see enormous potential in you, Jess, and I would see that in you even if you weren't God's daughter. So look, if you want to be the daughter of God, obviously you can be that. In fact, you have no choice in that matter just as I have no choice in Floyd Woodhouse, that mean old cuss, being *my* father. We don't get to pick our parents." Mrs. Thomas leaned forward the few necessary inches until she was on eye level with Jessica.

"But if you want to go in a different direction, if you

want to build a life completely independent from who your parents are, one that has nothing to do with religion or spirituality, you're strong enough to do that, too." Now she squatted down so that she looked up into Jessica's face. "You hear me? You can be whomever you want to be. You can do whatever you wish with your life. You're *not* defined by who your parents are. None of us are."

As appealing as that idea sounded, and as hungry for it as she was, Jess's gut immediately doubted its accuracy. No matter what she did, people found ways to drag either her mom or her dad into it. It was like everyone (except for Miranda and Mrs. Thomas, of course) either told her to be ashamed because of her mother or felt she was casting judgment upon them because of her father.

Until that moment, she hadn't understood how fully enmeshed she'd become in a no-win situation. No matter how she behaved, she was held hostage by one or both of her parents' reputation.

Blooming concurrently to that realization was a new, forbidden fantasy full of vivid detail: her life as an ordinary human girl. Maybe her mother was, say, a teacher (no reason), and her father was a respectable banker. Maybe she played sports and lived in a home suitable for sleepovers.

Imagining such a life felt good, even as it created a deep longing she knew she couldn't satisfy. That wasn't her life. Perhaps God could make it her life in an instant (seriously, she needed to get a handle on the extent of His powers), but He never would.

So perhaps there was a compromise. A middle ground.

One where she could keep her parents without living in their almighty shadows. What if she could learn to keep God out of her head or at least ignore Him when He popped on by? What if she could find a way to distance herself from Destinee's reputation and occasionally poor judgment?

It was the first bit of hope Jess had felt in weeks, even if it came with a hearty side of guilt.

She nodded and Mrs. Thomas stood. "Good. Then you need to head to lunch and get some food in you ... if you can stomach it after that slideshow."

Chapter Fifteen

"So how was sex ed, baby?" Destinee sat down at the kitchen table with her plate of fried chicken and looked eagerly at her daughter, who sat in her usual spot opposite.

Jess wished her mother hadn't asked her about sex ed while her cheeks were packed with chicken and sweet peas. An image from the slideshow surfaced in her mind, and she opened her mouth and used her tongue to force the half-chewed lump of food out onto her plate. She stared down at it, all fleshy and green. "Awful."

"At least you have spring break to recover."

Jess nodded noncommittally. "I guess."

"What'd I tell you about that slideshow? I called it, didn't I?" Destinee gnawed into her chicken leg, tearing off a large chunk and poking it all the way into her mouth with her finger. She sucked in air to combat the scalding meat, then gave in and sipped her beer as a last resort.

Jess rolled her eyes and nodded. "Yeah, you called it."

"And I bet you didn't learn a thing, either," she said around her food.

"Actually, we learned a lot."

Destinee stopped chewing to take a hard look at her daughter. "Really?"

Jess nodded and spooned a few peas into her mouth while trying her best not to think about herpes.

"Like what?"

"That sex should be respectful and between two consenting individuals." That particular lesson made perfect sense to Jess, which was always an added bonus in her education. She refrained from mentioning that it was God who'd taught it to her. She didn't want to give Him the credit and self-satisfaction.

But Destinee eyed her suspiciously and took another quick swig of beer. "Really? You learned about that today? In abstinence sex ed?"

Jess nodded. "Yeah. And that it shouldn't involve non-human animals."

Destinee nodded seriously and shook her chicken leg at Jess for emphasis. "That is very true. Screwing animals is a big no-no." She took another bite and then shoved the chicken into her cheek so she could speak around it. "And what about marriage?"

"Sex without consent within a marriage is still rape."

"Huh!" Destinee pouted out her lips and nodded approvingly. "Well isn't that something! Abstinence sex ed ain't what it used to be, I guess."

"Well, it wouldn't have been as good if Mrs. Thomas

didn't kick out the woman from White Light Church about halfway through."

Destinee's eyebrows shot up. "Did she really? Never thought much of that woman, but it sounds like she has some sense in her after all. So then Mrs. Thomas just taught it?"

"No. A doctor did. Dr. Fractal."

Now Destinee really seemed to think Jess was making things up. "Fractal, eh? I don't suppose she's related to Jameson Fractal."

How did everyone but Jess know who that was? "Yeah, his sister."

Destinee smacked the table. "Well, I'll be!"

"Who is he?"

"You kidding me?" Destinee tilted back the bottle, finishing off her beer.

"No."

"Jess, you really need to watch something other than nature shows. Every girl your age should know who Jameson Fractal is."

"Well, who is he?"

"Hell if I know what he actually does. But he's famous. He's … a celebrity. Maybe a little bit older than you. Eighteen maybe?"

That seemed a *lot* older.

"But he's cute, apparently. A little young for my taste—I like 'em older. Significantly older, obviously. But he's right up your alley. You crushing on boys yet?"

Jess's mind flickered to Chris. "No."

"Give it a year, then."

Destinee set her chicken leg down, wiped the grease from her mouth with her forearm, and then headed over to the fridge to grab another beer.

Jess mind traveled back to Chris's face when she'd smote the lightbulb above his head. What was the point of crushing on a guy if every guy she knew was scared of her because she was the daughter of God?

Mrs. Thomas's idea of being something other than just God's daughter sounded more and more appealing each time Jess considered it. Maybe if she told her mother about the idea, she would help her do it. (She'd leave out the part about distancing herself from Destinee, obviously.) Her mother never knew her own father, so who better to consult about a fatherless existence? Destinee might have all kinds of helpful hints.

Jessica pulled off a tiny chunk of chicken with her fingers and flicked it into her mouth, glancing up at her mother, who was back at the table again, going to town on her meal with a fresh beer in one hand and the chicken leg in the other.

It wasn't like Destinee was getting much out of God as the father of her child. It was settled. Jessica would broach the subject, see what she could pick from her mother's brain.

"Mom, can I talk to you about something?"

Concern crinkled the corners of Destinee's eyes as she paused in her chewing. "Of course, baby. Anything. Always."

Jessica filled her lungs with air. What she was about to say felt like crossing a line she couldn't uncross, but she doubted she'd regret it. "I don't think I want to be the daughter of God anymore."

Destinee dropped the chicken bone onto her plate, set the beer down slowly, leaned across the table, and smacked Jess on the side of the head with a greasy hand.

"Ow! What?"

Destinee swallowed her food. "That's for being an idiot. First of all, you don't have a choice about who your daddy is, and you should be glad you have one to begin with. What's more, you got about the best daddy around, even if he's almost never here and doesn't pay child support."

"But you're always complaining about him!"

"Course I am! That's what people do! They complain about their baby daddies and they curse God. I get to save myself trouble by doing both at the same time. That don't mean I wish he weren't around or I hate him. It's just what people do."

"It's awful, though! The kids at school hate me for it. They won't talk about things around me because they're afraid I'll tattle on them to God."

"Hm," said Destinee, leaning back in her chair. "These kids sound like idiots. You sure you *want* to be their friend?"

"Duh! But as long as I'm God's daughter, they'll never like me."

"What about Miranda?"

"Except for Miranda," Jessica amended.

Destinee sighed and shrugged a shoulder. "I don't know what to say, baby. You ain't got no choice about being God's daughter."

Okay, so her mother did *not* understand her dilemma. The sympathy she'd hoped for was nowhere to be found. Spitefully, she grumbled, "Mrs. Thomas says I can be whatever I want to be."

Destinee chuckled. "Sure, as long as what you want to be is God's daughter. Otherwise, you're screwed. You got a good lot in life, and I'll be damned if you turn your back on it and settle for any less, you understand me?"

Jess poked at her peas with her fork, and she could feel her mother's eyes still glued to her. "Yes."

But even as she said it, a new fantasy manifested in her mind's eye. What would life be like with a mother who actually listened to what Jess wanted? What would it be like to have a "cool" mom everyone loved and respected and never teased her about? A mom like, say, Mrs. Thomas?

Something inside her chest ached for that, and even though she knew it was impossible, she let her mind drift away into a parallel reality where everything was the same, except Mrs. Thomas was her mother and her father had died in an earthquake in Asia when she was just a baby …

Chapter Sixteen

13 AGC

Nine girls sat huddled in a tight circle on a pallet of pillows, blankets, and sleeping bags that covered the entirety of Sandra's bedroom floor. They had every intention of staying awake on said pallet, gossiping and giggling, all night long. Jess tried not to think too hard about how she'd made the list, along with Emma, Courtney, Miranda, Stephanie, one of Sandra's neighbors, and two of Sandra's cousins of a similar age. What mattered was that Jess had received the coveted invite, so once school started again after the summer, she had an exclusive party to add to her growing social resume upon entering eighth grade. And maybe, just maybe, this would be the year where she managed to separate her reputation from those of her parents, make more friends, and become exponentially less killable.

That was the plan, at least.

Mrs. Thomas had bought just about every junk food imaginable for them to devour over the course of the evening. She'd also downloaded an R-rated movie for them to watch later on. While Jess still didn't quite understand the rating system, it was clear that allowing children to watch an R-rated movie was something only cool parents did.

The movie would come later, though. Currently, Sandra was surrounded by gift bags and prissily wrapped boxes as she concocted melodrama over which to open first. The rest of the guests humored her, clamoring over the order of reputations put on trial, though not in so many words.

"Oh my god, don't open mine first," Stephanie Lee declared when Sandra reached for a gift bag covered in cartoon doodles of beauty supplies with the handles tied together by a showy gold bow.

"Should I save it for last?" Sandra asked, grinning slyly.

"Oh my god, no way. That's so much pressure!" Stephanie replied, giggling nervously.

Sandra then hovered her hand over one gift after the next, each slight movement causing anxious chatter among the party guests.

Sandra was clearly getting high off the power she wielded, but Jessica forced herself to ignore it, stamping a toothy grin onto her face.

It was, after all, Sandra's birthday party. If there were ever a time of year when someone was allowed to abuse their power, it seemed like their birthday was the obvious choice.

Unless that person was Jessica herself.

It's not even her actual birthday, Jessica thought bitterly, watching as Sandra finally grabbed a small box that Miranda claimed as her gift. While it was Sandra's birthday party, her actual birthday fell the Tuesday before. This was Saturday.

Saturday the seventh of July.

Jessica's birthday.

But no one outside of Miranda knew that tidbit.

"Okay, next! Who's this one from?" Sandra asked, holding up a turquoise gift bag with pink tissue paper blooming from the top.

Jessica's stomach dropped. "Mine."

She held her breath as Sandra pulled out the paper and stuck her hand blindly into the bag. "Oh, wow," she said, staring down at the colorful pallet of eyeshadow in her palm. "This is actually exactly what I wanted." While she didn't bother disguising the shock in her voice, of genuine appreciation made it go down smoother.

Jessica let out the breath she'd been holding and nodded. "Great! I just guessed," she lied.

The previous Sunday, Mrs. Thomas had emailed a picture of the exact item to Destinee with the subject line, *In case Jessica needs gift ideas.* It just so happened that the pharmacy, where Destinee had been working when she'd received the email, stocked the exact product. So her mom, who might have been more excited about Jessica's first sleepover than Jessica was, had done all the work, bringing home the eyeshadow already in the gift bag.

Sandra looked at Jessica with a new degree of respect. "That's awesome. Thanks!"

Jessica beamed. She was awesome. Scanning the circle of girls to make sure they were taking note of Jessica's awesomeness, her eyes landed on Miranda, who arched an unimpressed brow that brought Jessica right back down to earth.

Oh right. Miranda knew about the hot email tip.

Didn't matter. None of the other girls knew.

The sheer amount of damage control Jess's reputation required after the little sex-ed fiasco had instilled within her a heightened sense of cautiousness when it came to mentioning anything relating to God or her personal life.

But there was one detail she guarded more doggedly than any other. And that was her birthday.

Ever since she'd realized many years prior that Christmas and the insanity that went along with it was a celebration of her half-brother's birthday, she'd made a concerted effort to keep the date of her nativity under wraps. Every bit of public fussing about her birthday would only make it more difficult for her to distance herself from the two people who made her birth possible. She'd worked *too hard* and kissed *too much ass* in the last four months to let that happen.

So she reminded herself, as Sandra tore into her presents, gasping and squealing with unrestrained excitement, that forgoing recognition and gifts was a small but worthwhile price to pay for having friends.

Sandra ripped into the wrapping paper for the last of her presents, shucking it off and tossing it to the side of the pallet, and squealed at what she held in her hands. "Oh my god! Thank you, Emma!"

Jessica leaned to the side to get a better view, but she still couldn't get a good glimpse without crowding Courtney. "What is it?"

Sandra unfolded a ladies T-shirt and held it up for the rest of the girls to see. Jess read it. *Never the same. Never that different.* And behind the jagged text was the soulful face of everyone's favorite heartthrob, who she now recognized, thanks to a thorough Google search over spring break.

"I'm *so* jealous!" proclaimed Sandra's cousin Tracy. The girl looked just like Sandra, except her forehead was much too large in Jess's opinion. Or maybe her eyes were too low … "I saw that shirt online and was like, 'Oh my god, I have to have it.' I'm like, *so* jealous."

Sandra hugged it to her. "I love it! Thanks so much, Emma!"

"Did you see *Cutthroat Times* yet?" Emma asked.

"No, but that's what my mom downloaded for tonight!" Sandra said.

Tracy and Sandra's other cousin, Natalia, who was only a grade ahead of them but at least a foot and a half taller, squealed and flapped their hands. "Oh my god no way!"

But Emma remained calm and collected. "I mean, it's good but it's not his best. *Bridge to November* is way better."

"Well, duh," Sandra said, holding up the shirt as evidence, and Jess could only surmise that the Jameson Fractal quote on the front of it—which made zero sense to her, if she were honest—was from that particular movie.

After her comprehensive image search of the well-known heartthrob, Jess had decided two things. First, Jameson Fractal was cute, with his dark blond hair, hazel eyes, and leather jackets, but she by no means had a crush on him. Second, she must never let any of her friends know she didn't have a crush on Jameson Fractal. And while she'd done her homework to an extent, she hadn't actually taken the extra step of watching him in any of his movies, so when that topic arose, as it frequently did, she nodded enthusiastically—but not too enthusiastically—with each opinion that was expressed.

"Yeah, *Bridge to November* is a good one." She murmured it just loud enough for it to register on Emma's radar so that the girl glanced over and nodded approvingly but not so loud that anyone would remember her claiming to have seen it later on if she was directly asked about it.

"Cake's ready!" Mrs. Thomas hollered from the kitchen.

"Sweet!" Sandra stood and slipped her new shirt on over her head. "My mom bakes the best cake, you guys. Like, seriously."

They followed Sandra out into the kitchen where her ten-year-old brother, Fischer, was sitting at the table, kicking his legs back and forth under his chair. Fischer, in general, reminded Jess of a ticking time bomb. He regularly made Sandra look well-mannered and charitable by comparison. Jess couldn't stand him and, for whatever reason, he also couldn't stand her. It was like he bristled up every time she got near him, and sometimes he even went as far as to single her out from the group as a target for his annoying behavior.

"Mom! Fischer just stuck his finger in the icing!" Sandra smacked him, and he tried to hit her back, but she dodged his reach.

"Fischer," Mrs. Thomas said, sounding irritated like she usually did with him. "Go away. Get out of here. Go play video games or something."

"Mom …" he whined.

"No. It's your sister's party. Get out of here."

Jessica admired Mrs. Thomas for her direct approach with the brat of a child, even if he was her own. It was like he wasn't even trying to be loved. Nothing about that mentality made any sense to her.

The guests circled around the table and Mrs. Thomas lit all thirteen candles with a Bic lighter.

"Mom, do you like my new shirt?" Sandra pulled on the bottom of it so that the whole text and picture were flat and visible.

Mrs. Thomas looked over at it once the candles were lit. "Ooh. Sexy!" she said, wiggling her hips playfully. That made everyone giggle, including Mrs. Thomas herself, which was startling. Jess couldn't remember seeing or hearing her former teacher giggle.

It made Jess love her even more than she already did, and Emma whispered, "Her mom's so cool," to Courtney, who smiled but looked to be in the throes of extreme spiritual conflict.

Sandra made a wish and blew out all but three of the candles on her first try, leaving a perfect little triangle in the center of the cake.

"Guess you were only supposed to be ten this year," Mrs. Thomas joked. When Jessica looked at her, she was smiling, but it looked a little forced.

Maybe Mrs. Thomas doesn't even like Sandra that much.

It was a comforting thought that someone as cool and popular as Mrs. Thomas might like Jess more than her own daughter.

Mrs. Thomas cut into the cake and began plating the pieces and passing them around in a circle until each guest had the slice she wanted.

Sandra hadn't been exaggerating; Mrs. Thomas baked one heck of a cake. This one in particular was a masterpiece. Buttercream frosting with green icing flowers in small bunches, over what seemed to be alternating layers of angel food cake, more buttercream, and blueberry jam. Was there lemon too? Jess had never tasted cake this good, and she'd definitely never found a cake *interesting* before.

Even Mrs. Thomas couldn't refuse it and served herself a large piece that she devoured quickly. After licking some rogue icing off her thumb and then wiping her hands off on a stiff pink party napkin, Mrs. Thomas perked up as she addressed the partygoers with, "You want me to start the movie?"

The reply was a resounding yes.

All nine girls managed to fit onto the white leather sectional sofa, cake in lap, to watch the movie. Jess hadn't the slightest idea what *Cutthroat Times* was about, and halfway through it, she *still* wasn't entirely sure. She did, however, understand two things: First, *Cutthroat Times* was the most violent movie she'd ever seen. Second, Jameson Fractal was without a doubt the hottest man on earth. She got it now. The pictures on the Internet didn't do him justice, not even a little bit.

She came to the second realization about two seconds into his first sex scene with his love interest, who was supposed to be a singer or a dancer or maybe a spy?—that part of the plot was still unclear. Dr. Fractal's technical explanations had made the act of sex seem like a joyless medical experiment requiring focus and precision. But that wasn't what this scene with Dr. Fractal's little brother felt like by any means. This sex scene was recklessness, passion, some slapping—which seemed odd—and shirt-tearing, but mostly thrusting. So much thrusting. So many different angles of it, too. There was sweat, as well. And not as much use of a bed as Jess had expected.

Even as she sat motionless on the couch, her heart raced, threatening to spring free of her ribcage. Because she was absolutely terrified. *That* was sex? That seemed like something that could easily result in an accidental death. But, based on the sounds Jameson's singer-or-dancer-or-maybe-spy love interest was making, sex also seemed like it could result in the most amazing feeling that could happen to anyone ever.

She tried to imagine herself in place of the brunette actress, but her mind shied away from that; the idea of being manhandled by someone as gorgeous as Jameson Fractal short-circuited her imagination. She wondered briefly if his big sister had ever watched this film, but judging from Dr. Fractal's dry, clinical outlook on sex, that seemed unlikely.

All cake eating had ceased on the sectional sofa, all movement as well. A tingling began to gather in her lower abdomen, just above her lady bits, and she wondered if this was what an orgasm was. Probably not. The intensity of it didn't match what she knew of the concept. And when she saw the writhing brunette presumably experience an on-screen orgasm while being pinned between Jameson Fractal and a brick wall as she huffed and puffed and moaned and yelled, Jess decided that she hadn't just had one herself. The tightening of her muscles must be something else. It *was* intensifying, but when she tuned into it, she decided it wasn't intensifying in a particularly pleasant way.

Finally, the scene ended and the movie carried on with whatever sinewy plot it pretended to have. But Jessica didn't bother herself much with following along. She wanted to watch the sex scene over and over again until she could get a handle on it. She grappled with whether she would ever feel comfortable doing that with someone, despite how part of her actively wanted to do that with Jameson Fractal himself.

In the end, she couldn't imagine being that woman. She would feel silly doing that. She didn't like being loud, for one. But at the same time, she wished she were a person who *could* do that without feeling silly. A sexy person.

If she ever were to get herself into a situation like the one she'd just seen on the TV, though, God would most likely interrupt anyway and ruin everything, as he was known to do whenever she was particularly enjoying herself. So there was that.

Jess continued her struggle to comprehend the on-screen action as Jameson orchestrated a heist—or maybe a rescue or a party or something. But suddenly she was hit out of nowhere with a wave of lightheadedness. Then the tingling in her brain turned into pressure behind her eyes, and the place in her belly where she'd felt her passion amass only minutes before ached in earnest. She wondered if the cake wasn't sitting well with her, but she'd had food not sit well with her before, and it'd never left her cramping *quite* like this.

While she ran through a list of possible diagnoses for her sudden symptoms, rain began to fall outside the living room window, flicking at the glass and stomping on the roof. It was a moment before her mind officially registered it, by which time the wind was blowing torrentially, causing large drops to beat against the pane like they were frantically begging for entry.

She felt something stab her temple so hard, she whipped her head toward Miranda, thinking her friend had jabbed her with a finger. But Miranda was still glued to the movie, her focused expression suggesting that she was struggling as much as Jess had been to follow the convoluted plotline. It was the same expression Miranda donned whenever a new concept was explained in math— her eyes squinted to slits, her nose crinkled around the edges, her upper lip raised to reveal her two large front teeth. Clearly, it hadn't been Miranda who'd caused the pain in Jessica's temple. Maybe Jess was really sick. Maybe she should call up her mom and go home.

No. This was an important sleepover. God wouldn't allow her to suffer a stroke and keel over. Probably. She would push through it.

During a strange, bloody fight scene, where she couldn't tell who was punching whom, lightning lit up the living room through the window a split second before the power went out. The girls were jolted from their fantasy, and on Jessica's left, Courtney screamed.

"I'm scared of the dark!" she proclaimed, and Jess secretly hoped that admission would spell social destruction for the girl later on.

Once Mrs. Thomas arrived with flashlights and a battery-powered lantern, things started to settle down.

"It'll come back on in a second," she assured them, "and then you can finish your movie."

But almost immediately after she left the room to find more flashlights, hail started pounding on the window. No one would be stupid enough to repair downed power lines in Texas hail, which could intensify from high-velocity marbles to lethal grapefruits in a snap.

Sandra's cousins, the neighbor, and Stephanie whimpered softly, and Courtney, Emma, and Sandra took turns proclaiming how each was the most scared of hail out of the bunch.

The lightning that struck the tree in the backyard put a quick stop to all the blubbering, though. Through the window, Jess saw its jagged flash a millisecond before the deafening crack of thunder caused her to jump in her seat. And when she did, she felt something wet and sloshy in her pajama shorts. Had she peed herself? Surely not.

"Oh my god! It's on fire!" Emma yelled, pointing at the tree.

Jess turned her attention back to the window to see that the large oak had been split in two and was burning between the halves, though the rain was preventing the flames from spreading.

"Oh my god! Why is this happening to me?" Sandra wailed through tears.

At the mention of her Father, Jess couldn't help but wonder if all this—the cramping and the sudden extreme weather conditions—had something to do with Him. Wrath? Was this the punishment for lust? That didn't sound like Him. That didn't sound like Him at all.

God ... God!

No reply.

Ugh. Typical.

Jess made to stand up, but as soon as she shifted, she was reminded of the moisture from before, which was still pressed against her. *Had* she peed her pants? She hadn't *felt* all that scared by the strange weather ...

With only cheap flashlights that no one could seem to hold steady and a dim lantern illuminating the room, and with all the girls' attention focused out the window, maybe she could sneak to the bathroom without anyone noticing.

She stood slowly, clenching to make sure she didn't accidentally pee more, and then turned to see if she'd left anything behind on the sectional. Her mind hardly had any time to reconcile what she'd expected to see with what was actually there before Sandra's eyes landed upon it too, and she squealed, "Oh my god! Blood! Ewww!"

Blood? Why was she ... ? Oh.

Maybe it was because Dr. Fractal had so recently occupied real estate in her brain, but Jess put the pieces together immediately.

But *really*? At a sleepover? On her birthday? In front of everyone else?

Well, when she thought about it like that, she probably should have expected this from the get-go.

She stared at the small pool of blood on the leather cushion and watched resignedly as the liquid fanned out to cover more surface area.

She was so preoccupied with watching the slow progress of it that she overlooked an important logical conclusion: if she bled onto the couch, the blood had passed through the cloth of her shorts, leaving visible evidence there as well. Courtney didn't overlook that, though, and she leaned at a severe angle to get a glimpse of Jess's butt before loudly drawing everyone's attention to it. As the rain quenched the last of the tree fire, the commotion outside was forgotten, lost in a cacophony of squeals, laughter, and chatter.

Jess felt her face flush crimson. Where to go from there? Should she sit back down? Should she embrace it and laugh along with them? Should she go sprinting for the bathroom to wait things out until she could come up with a better plan?

Yeah, that would do.

She tried to snatch the flashlight from Emma's hand, but the girl's grip was surprisingly strong, and Jess ended up in a struggle with her for control of it.

"Hey! Hey!" Mrs. Thomas was back in the living room. "Everybody calm down! What's going on here?"

"Jessica bled on the sofa," Sandra said, pointing at the spot.

Jess let go of the flashlight as strength drained from her muscles, like someone had draped a dozen lead blankets over her head and shoulders.

Everybody knew.

Maybe they hadn't made the leap of connecting the start of her period to the freak weather, which *she'd* guessed immediately, but they all knew that she had started her period, and that was humiliating enough.

Mrs. Thomas looked at where her daughter pointed, frowned for a moment, then looked back up at Sandra. "So? I don't get why that's something to make such a big deal about. Every woman gets her period, and every woman, at some point or another wasn't expecting it."

She turned to Miranda. "Would you grab a wet paper towel from the kitchen?" Miranda nodded and ran out. "The rest of you—it's time for bed. The electricity might not be back on for a while, so it looks like we'll have to finish the rest of the movie in the morning."

The last thing Jessica wanted to do was to be locked away in Sandra's bedroom with the other girls, but luckily she wouldn't have to be, because Mrs. Thomas added, "Jessica, you stay with me." In different circumstances, with a different adult, she would have assumed that meant she was in trouble, but not with Mrs. Thomas.

Sandra's mother knelt down and assured Jess that there was nothing to be embarrassed about. "You know," she said, "the last Wednesday before we went to summer break, I had to leave Marymoore early because I started my period unexpectedly and bled through my khakis."

That somehow made Jess feel a little better, even while

it grossed her out thinking about Mrs. Thomas on her period.

"You just have to keep an extra change of underwear and maybe a skirt or shorts in your backpack for when it happens again," she coached. "Luckily, it's the summer, so you have some time to get a hang of it before you go back to school."

It was sound advice. And while Jess had long suspected that Mrs. Thomas was one of her angels, her help in such a horrifying situation as this served as welcome confirmation. The only question was whether the woman knew she was an angel or if she still hadn't figured it out.

When Miranda returned, Jess took the paper towels from her and wiped down the leather couch. The blood came off easily, which was a relief. Now all she needed was to get out of these shorts.

"Come with me," Mrs. Thomas said. "I'm going to show you how to deal with all this. Miranda, would you go grab Jess a change of pants from her bag?"

"Yep." Miranda hurried off to Sandra's bedroom, and Mrs. Thomas led Jess to the bathroom.

Mrs. Thomas pulled a brightly colored cardboard box out from under the sink and then pulled out a little wrapped pouch. Once the packaging was off it, Jess recognized it from sex ed. "Sandra still hasn't started her period. She's a little bit behind on … well, everything." Mrs. Thomas chuckled, so Jess chuckled too.

She held out the box and added, "You know, it's really not the end of the world, even if it feels like it. Just don't let it get to you. I know you must feel like the weight of the world is on your shoulders, but that doesn't mean you have to think about it all day, every day. You can still have fun and be a teenager. I promise nothing terrible will happen if you occasionally cut yourself a break and focus on things that make you happy."

Jessica wasn't sure what Mrs. Thomas was talking about specifically, but the words struck a chord inside her nonetheless. She sighed and nodded, forcing a smile and hoping it caused her mood to adjust in kind.

After a quick refresher on how to actually use a pad, wings and all, Mrs. Thomas left Jess to it, but not before asking, "You want me to call your mom and have her pick you up once the weather lets up a bit?"

"Yeah, I don't feel good."

Mrs. Thomas nodded. "You should go home and do something that makes you feel better, whatever that is." She pressed her lips together into a concerned smile and then shut the bathroom door behind her. When Jess heard a small knock on the door a minute later, she opened it to find Miranda standing there, holding Jess's jeans and a clean pair of underwear. "I started mine last year," she said.

"Really?" Jess asked, astounded. How had she not known this about her best friend?

"Yeah. It's not that bad. It's just … a hassle."

Jess wasn't sure what else to say, so she took her clothes from Miranda and thanked her.

"I told them to cut it out," Miranda added. "They promised not to say anything to anyone. And I do too."

"Thanks." Jess appreciated the thought, but wondered if

it was too much to hope for that Miranda wouldn't let slip about her birthday *or* her period.

She closed the bathroom door and went to work.

Once she'd carefully stuck the pad to the inside of her underwear, she took two steps forward before the horror sank in. A *hassle*? This was like wearing a diaper!

She closed the toilet lid and sat down on it, putting her head in her hands. She felt like crying, but no tears came. Then she tried to internalize Mrs. Thomas's advice, but amid the swarm of emotions, that wasn't happening either. So she distracted herself with mental math, and it was some small comfort: at least she only had to start her period around 240 more times before someone would eventually kill her.

Chapter Seventeen

Jess pretended not to notice that Destinee was staring unblinkingly at her across the kitchen table. She had enough anxieties flopping around in her mind on this first day of eighth grade without having to worry about her mother's concerns on top of that.

And Jess was back on her period. If she'd thought the lightning storm at Sandra's house had been bad, it was nothing compared to the natural disaster that had torn through Mooretown and the surrounding counties two nights before.

She ladled a large spoonful of oatmeal into her mouth, adjusted in her seat in a futile attempt to make the pad more comfortable, and hoped that her mother would stop staring soon.

"You heard from him lately?" Destinee asked.

"No. Not directly."

Destinee nodded, but didn't seem satisfied. "It just seems like he'd make an appearance after ... you know."

Jessica did indeed know, thanks to News 9 out of Midland, whose Sunday morning coverage included the strange string of weather events that began roughly to the minute of Jess bleeding and lasted into Saturday night, ending around the time Jess's day-one cramping ceased at four in the morning. Though a small twister had touched down just west of Big Spring, yet again it was the lightning that caused most of the chaos. Thirteen head of cattle had dropped over dead when a bolt struck the ground near them—a bit of bad luck that was made extra noteworthy by the fact that the cows were standing next to a large metal tower with a lightning rod extending upward from it. The town of Andrews had even suffered three human fatalities from lightning strikes … though by lunchtime, news stations were announcing that all three deceased men had been serial sex offenders. The well-placed lightning wasn't mentioned on the evening news, seemingly forgotten about, which was usually the fate of any story that left most viewers *less* frightened to set foot outside their homes.

Then that evening, on the six o'clock news, the anchor introduced his special remote guest, Reverend Dean, and Jess asked Destinee to please, for the love of all things, turn off the TV. The last person she wanted providing color commentary on events related to her period was Jimmy, that backstabbing fraud.

But Destinee had refused, saying, "The devil you know …"

Jess assumed it was a figure of speech because, despite his many flaws, she was still fairly certain that Jimmy Dean was not the Devil. Why would God enlist the help of His adversary to find His daughter on the night of her birth? Duh, He wouldn't.

On the TV, Jimmy stood under the White Light archway, dressed to the nines in his white suit and pig-hoof stole. He nodded along with the reporter on scene as she introduced him and mentioned a few of the strange events that had happened. Jimmy just did Jimmy. *Sin! Lowly animals! Punishment!* And then he said one word that hadn't yet crossed Jessica's mind: *Apocalypse.*

She'd watched a special on the wildlife of ancient Mesoamerica, and through learning about Mayans, she'd also gleaned a few things about the end of the world. It seemed like a strange thing for a culture to be obsessed with. But regardless of what Jimmy might claim, she felt pretty sure this wasn't the end of days. God would have told her, right?

As she'd watched Jimmy on the news the night before, she'd concluded that this was the worst possible way for anyone to be welcomed into womanhood.

She hurried and finished her breakfast to escape her mother's intense stare, and then ran to her bedroom to finish getting ready for school. She tried to keep from imagining the million possible scenarios resulting from someone at the party spreading word around school that Jess had bled on Sandra Thomas's couch.

It'd been just over a month since that incident, so maybe there was a chance the girls at the party had done so many other fun things (none of which she was invited to) they'd forgotten all about her bloody faux pas.

She grabbed her backpack off the bed, checked to make sure she had enough pads tucked into the front pocket, and then heaved the bag over her shoulder and took a deep breath to relax. Having a period was natural—so why did it feel shameful and disgusting? She would have asked God about that, but He hadn't shown His face since she'd officially entered womanhood, and she suspected He would find an excuse to avoid talking about it even if He *did* decide to show up.

The walk from her house to Marymoore Junior High was just shy of fifteen minutes. She left extra early this morning, though, to make sure she gave herself a cushion, just in case Saturday night's storms had caused any damage on her route that might make it slow going. Since most of her journey was along dirt roads until she reached the square, the need for alternate routes was likely.

But the August sun had dried up most of the mud, and she managed to avoid the worst of it, sparing her white sneakers until she was finally home-free on the concrete sidewalks of Mooretown's small square.

The square functioned as her social warm-up before she hit the rowdy halls of Marymoore. She knew each of the adults who owned the quaint shops—many she'd known since she was a baby, with only a few newcomers to the town—and most of them didn't believe she was the Antichrist. Some were even friendly and waved or said good morning to her as she passed.

Mrs. Mathers, a lady in perhaps her early fifties who owned a small bakery just off the main square, had a special motherly kind of affection for Jess and snuck her warm yeast rolls on the way to school each morning. It was one of the few things that excited Jess about starting school again after the summer, and it was an unnecessary act of kindness that had helped her slog through her seventh grade year. When Jess had mentioned Mrs. Mathers's generosity to her mother toward the end of the previous school year, Destinee had informed her that she and Mrs. Mathers's son Denton had hooked up a handful of times their junior year of high school and Mrs. Mathers had disapproved passionately.

"I'm glad to hear she's come around, though," Destinee had added.

But that insight had immediately put things into perspective for Jess, who happened to know via the Divine Grapevine that Denton now had five children by five different women and was among the most virile human men walking the face of the earth. When the two bits of intel were set next to each other, it became obvious that Mrs. Mathers assumed Jess was her illegitimate granddaughter.

The rolls were so good, though, Jess never bothered setting the record straight.

But as she hobbled to school with the pad rubbing her awkwardly each step of the way—*Surely everyone has to be able to tell I'm wearing this*—even Mrs. Mathers's warm roll couldn't lift her spirits. It must have been obvious, because when Jess accepted the roll with a small thank you, Mrs. Mathers frowned. "Hold on. I know what you need." She returned with a croissant and handed it to Jess, who smiled, thanked her again, and waddled onward.

Once she'd finished her yeast roll and bit into the croissant a block down from the bakery, she realized that it wasn't *just* a croissant. It was a jelly-filled croissant. When she held it at arm's length to see the strawberry jelly dribbling out of it, her stomach churned and she struggled to swallow down the bite she already had in her mouth before tossing the rest of it into the next trashcan she saw.

Could Mrs. Mathers be the Devil? she wondered. *No. Stop thinking about the Devil. You have more important things to worry about today.*

Jess waddled into school, hoping her gait didn't look the way it felt: like she'd been riding a horse around for days. Sleeping in a pad with a heavy flow had left her tossing and turning all night, and she'd woken up in the morning with small bits of chafing on her inner thighs where the wings had rubbed. She clenched her jaw against the rawness around her panty line as she tried to walk normally for the length of the hallway to her first class. As she hoped to find a friendly face, she realized that she didn't even know who that might be outside of Miranda. Maybe Emma or Sandra?

And finding one became even less likely when she realized that people were staring at her as she passed by them in the hallway, whispering behind their hands and giggling. Really? School hadn't even started and word had already gotten around? That seemed too unfair.

Maybe she was just being paranoid. Surely, she wasn't the only girl currently saddled with a sandpaper pillow.

How long is this freaking hallway?

It seemed to stretch on forever, and the eighth-grade

hall was at the very back of the school, leaving her an even farther distance to traverse before she could be safely seated in her advanced English class.

Destinee had assured her that most girls start their period by eighth grade. Whether that was actually true or not was debatable, because Destinee was no Dr. Fractal. But Jess would function off of that assumption for the sake of being able to run some numbers …

There were about sixty girls in eighth grade at Marymoore. Say seventy percent had already started their period. That was forty-two girls who had probably started their period in eighth grade alone. Now, one week a month meant that at any given time, a quarter of those girls were probably on their period. So one-quarter of forty-two was about ten. Minus Jess. So about nine other eighth-grade girls at Marymoore were probably on their period.

The mental math carried her until she was in the eighth-grade hallway, at which point she made it her mission to pick out the other nine bleeding girls by the way they were walking and standing. She let herself become obsessed with it, and it proved useful in helping her continue to put one foot in front of the other all the way to her classroom.

Almost none of her friends had qualified for the early start high school classes, but Destinee had pressured Jess into taking the necessary tests at the end of seventh grade, and she'd unfortunately passed them with flying colors. So that meant she had to find new friends or risk being a loner, which, as appealing as it sounded at times, meant that she would find herself bullied by both the kids who didn't place into the advanced courses *and* the kids who did. She needed as many allies as she could get if this year was going to be bearable. And things already weren't looking great for her.

The worst part was the Wursts. Both Courtney *and* Trent had tested into the advanced classes, and while Courtney by herself could sometimes be tolerable, when she was with her twin brother and Emma wasn't around, the twins immediately reverted to their monstrous selves. Yet another reason Jess needed to find new allies and quick.

"Good morning, Jessica," said Ms. Cantos from her post just outside the classroom door. She was perhaps a few years out of college and, with her short, dark bob, thick eyelashes, and silky tan skin, reminded Jessica of a modern Cleopatra. Except Jessica suspected she was Hispanic rather than Egyptian.

They'd met briefly on the registration day over the summer, and Jessica hadn't expected the teacher to remember her. Despite how many townsfolk knew Jessica's name, she always assumed that she was forgettable. She held these two beliefs side by side without feeling inclined to pick a winner: too many people knew her name, and yet she was forgettable. Low self-esteem for the win.

"Morning, Ms. Cantos."

"Sit wherever you like, Jessica." The woman smiled like she'd just bestowed some sort of privilege rather than passing a bleak sentence. Free seating might be nice for people who had friends in the class, but for people like her, it was a subtle form of torture. Often, it presented itself like a logic puzzle. Sitting next to someone meant aligning

seat before a sideways glance at Greg caused her to pause.

The expression was only there for a split second before he smoothed it away, but it was unmistakable. She'd witnessed it too many times to not recognize when juicy gossip about her was surfacing in someone's mind. Maybe it was the slight lifting of the eyelids, a crinkle of the top lip just below the nostrils, a downtick of the lips at the corners.

It wasn't hard to guess what had flashed in Greg's mind: the couch incident. She should've known better than to think a month was enough time for something that incriminating to pass out of the gossip circuit.

Jessica rolled her eyes and scooted right back out from behind her desk. But Greg put a hand on her backpack and stopped her. "What is it?" he asked. His round face stared up at her from underneath this short, curly dark-chocolate hair. She shot him a look that she hoped expressed her incredulity. "You know what."

"Okay, look," he said quietly. "Yeah, I heard about it like everyone else did. But don't worry, I'm not going to be weird about it. I've read all about that stuff in books and online forums, and I know it's normal."

She placed her palm not so gently onto her face. He was just making it worse. "I just … Can we not talk about it?"

He nodded. "Yeah. Sure."

She sighed and sat down next to him. As he returned his attention to the book in his hand, she waited awkwardly and anxiously for the rest of the class to file in.

Jess had never talked to a boy about sex stuff. Granted, bleeding from the vagina seemed like the opposite of sex itself, but it was still something involving lady parts, and she'd never thought a boy could talk about it so plainly.

But no calmness or reassurance from Greg could dismiss the fact that *someone* at Sandra's birthday party had been running her mouth. Not only had they told, but they had told so many people that even Greg, who didn't seem like the type to be up-to-date on gossip, knew. Miranda had made everyone at the party promise not to tell, but someone still had.

Could it have been Miranda? It did sound like something she would accidentally let slip. Jess had long since come to terms with the fact that her best friend was the one who God had foretold would constantly betray her that way, but it didn't make it sting any less each time it happened. Maybe this time it would be someone else who'd betrayed her, someone who did it on purpose; that way Jess could let herself be angry.

So she decided to ignore the possibility of it being Miranda until she'd ruled out everything else.

Someone had told Greg about it, anyhow. If she really wanted to get to the bottom of it, she could simply ask him who he'd heard it from. But that would require bringing it up again.

Or she could hope God would swoop down into her head and enlighten her.

"Ha!" She didn't mean to laugh aloud, but the idea of God having timing that worked for *her* was literally laughable.

"What is it?" Greg asked.

Her mind was so set on avoiding the topic of

menstruation that it let an equally undesirable topic slip out: "Do you believe in God?" Definitely not ideal, but she couldn't take it back, and it might actually be helpful to know where she stood with Greg, if they were to become friends. She'd learned the hard way not to function off the assumption that just because God spoke to her meant He made Himself so obvious (and intrusive) in other people's lives.

Greg shifted uncomfortably in his seat. If he knew about her period, odds were he'd heard about her divinity. How could anyone in Mooretown not? But that *did* leave him between a rock and a hard place if he didn't believe in God.

Greg scrunched up his nose apologetically. "Um. I mean."

"It's okay if you don't," she assured him quickly. "There's actually no punishment for it as long as you're not a jerk about it."

Greg tilted his head slightly to the side. "I don't understand why you think that, but okay. No, I don't believe in God."

She grinned and let those words wash over her, pretending for a moment that she believed them. Something about that relaxed her to the point of sighing deeply. "Good. I mean, at least you know what you believe."

"Do *you* believe in God?" The nervousness in his voice was obvious, but he powered through it in a way that earned a little more of her respect.

"Yeah. Unfortunately. I wish I didn't." The taste of Mrs.

Mathers' warm rolls surfaced in her mouth. "Never mind." This topic had quickly turned less enjoyable than talking about her period. So, might as well …

"Who told you about my … about the party?"

He nodded slightly toward the row of desks two ahead of them, where Courtney and Trent now sat.

Jess felt like cheering, but she knew that would leave too much to explain to Greg, so she faked outrage and betrayal. But the fact that it was Courtney who had spread it around was actually fantastic for two reasons: it meant Miranda could still be her loyal best friend, but mostly, it gave Jessica another substantial reason to hate Courtney, which she'd craved for quite some time now. Maybe she could even leverage this to convince the rest of the girls who still insisted on being friends with Courtney that the girl should be ostracized.

Ms. Cantos put the daily agenda up on the projector, and the small sense of victory and hope that Jess had felt blossoming in her body vanished almost instantly.

Objective: How can a symbol be used to express multiple viewpoints?

Review: What is a symbol?

Warm up: Make a list of things that can be symbolized by blood.

Lesson: The importance of blood in 17th-century texts
1. Lady Macbeth—"Out, damned spot!"
2. Dante's Inferno—Phlegethon, the River of Blood

3. Machiavelli—Weakness of bloodlines
Essay topic: Select one of the above examples and compare the
notions of blood presented in the work with contemporary opinions
and views.

By the time Jess had read through the entire agenda, she was fairly certain that Ms. Cantos was a demon. Maybe not a Randy-level demon, but a demon nonetheless.

Once the bell signaled the start of class and students quieted down, Ms. Cantos moved to the whiteboard where the agenda was projected, folded her hands, and smiled. The young, petite Latina teacher was particularly pretty when she smiled, and Jess genuinely wished she wasn't definitely a demon.

After Ms. Cantos finished her introduction and a half-hearted apology about actually making them do work on the first day of school, followed by a pep talk on being in advanced classes and the responsibility that goes along with that, she turned her attention to the agenda. "I know how much you guys love a little gore, so I thought I'd throw you a bone on the first day of school." She wiggled her eyebrows at the class.

Jessica sighed.

Courtney raised her hand and Ms. Cantos called on her.

"Will we be reading any passages where someone bleeds through their pants at a birthday party?"

Ms. Cantos screwed up her face and tilted her head to the side. "I'm not sure ... Would you like to explain why you're asking?"

But the snickering was already in full swing, and Jess

could feel her face grow hot.

"Don't worry, Courtney," Greg said. "You'll become a woman someday. You can stop obsessing over it."

The collective snickering morphed into shocked, disbelieving cackling then, and even Jess wanted to laugh, though it was mostly from relief.

Ms. Cantos's head snapped toward him. "Greg! What ... What is going on here?"

Greg had just risked his status as Teacher Favorite by being mean without making Ms. Cantos laugh, that's what was going on. Jess looked at him with new eyes. He'd taken a bullet for her.

"Nothing, Ms. C. I'll explain after class."

She looked at him like he'd somehow betrayed her, like he'd reneged on some secret deal. "You bet you will. Okay, so back to the lesson."

Jess glanced at Greg, and he met her gaze. Her heart started to race, and she looked away.

Ms. Cantos began the PowerPoint, starting with Macbeth and working her way through. She was actually a pretty cool teacher.

Maybe she wasn't a demon.

But even with entrancing images of the Inferno projected onto the whiteboard, Jess wasn't able to focus on the lesson. Instead, she was completely preoccupied with the close proximity of her new atheist protector.

When it was time to pair up and brainstorm for the essay, Greg immediately turned toward her and cocked an eyebrow. She smiled and nodded. Maybe he was just being nice.

Or maybe he was the next best thing to Jameson Fractal. She wasn't sure yet.

What would a normal teenager do?

She would have a supermassive crush on Greg.

By the end of the class, Jessica was pretty certain she was in love with him. He waited for her to get her things and walked with her out of the classroom. But before they made it to the door, Ms. Cantos held out her arm and stopped him. She had her eyebrows raised, the corners of her mouth rounded into a slight frown as she waited for an explanation. Greg sighed and played the part of the repentant sinner, and Jess decided the least she could do was to hang back with him and help explain what was going on.

He led off with, "See, the thing is—"

"Greg was just standing up for me," she interrupted. She wanted to give credit where it was due, and explaining it to Ms. Cantos seemed a lot easier than actually thanking Greg directly. "I had, um, sort of a woman problem happen at Sandra Thomas's house over the summer, and everyone there promised not to say anything, but ..."

Ms. Cantos nodded slowly, comprehension dawning. "Ohh ... okay. Yeah, now that I think about it, I'd heard something along those lines, but I didn't realize it was about you."

"Greg was just standing up for me."

Ms. Cantos bit her lip and turned her eyes back to Greg. It almost looked like she was holding back a smile. "Okay, fair enough." Then she turned to Jess. "Sorry your friends are talking about that. I had something similar happen when I was about your age."

Jess wanted to ask, "Did it get people preaching about the apocalypse, too?" but she resisted because Ms. Cantos was just trying to make her feel better.

"Anyway, Emma shouldn't have told everyone about that," the teacher added.

Wait. Emma? Busty, queen bee Emma? "No, it was Courtney. Didn't Courtney tell you, Greg?"

Greg nodded. "Yeah. It definitely wasn't Emma. She wouldn't do that."

Ms. Cantos grimaced apologetically. "Um, well, yeah. Hate to say, Greg, but I overheard Emma telling people about it in the hallway today. Like I said, I didn't hear her mention Jess specifically, but I did hear the basic story coming from her mouth."

Greg's jaw went slack and his rosy cheeks lost some of their color. "I— I'll go talk to her about that."

Ms. Cantos pressed her lips together and nodded. "Okay, you do that." She turned to Jess. "If you need someone to bitch to, let me know."

While Jess appreciated the swearing, all she wanted to do was to get out of the classroom and find a reason to go home sick.

But then if word got out that she was sick, people might ask questions, and then *everyone* would end up finding out she was on her period.

Another no-win situation for Jessica McCloud. I bet Jesus never had to deal with junior high ...

"You two better go before you're late to class."

Jess nodded, put her head down and made straight for the door, not bothering to wait for Greg.

Miranda was already in natural sciences when Jess arrived, and she moved her backpack from the desk next to hers, which she'd saved for her best friend. Mr. Harrison was going over the daily agenda by the time Jess slipped into the classroom, so she headed over to her saved seat quietly, and quickly settled in.

"Why are you late?" Miranda whispered, looking concernedly at Jess.

"Apparently *some people* can't keep a dang secret." It wasn't by any means an adequate explanation, but Miranda accepted it as one nonetheless and squished up her face sympathetically.

"Sorry about that."

"You didn't tell anyone, did you?"

"No way. Not even accidentally."

Jess studied her for a moment and decided to believe her.

Then Miranda added, "I wouldn't betray you like stupid old Sandra."

"*Sandra?*"

"Yeah, she was telling people about it first period. I made her stop, though."

"Ladies in the back," Mr. Harrison said, interrupting himself mid-sentence. "Did you have something to contribute?"

"No, sir," Miranda replied. Mr. Harrison was the kind of teacher you called sir. He'd taught science for nineteen years, a tidbit Jessica had learned after Destinee looked at her class schedule the week before and exclaimed, *"That mean old bastard? He's still kicking? Huh. Figured he'd've had a heart attack by now."*

So maybe it was Miranda's small sign of respect or the fact that it was still early on in the first day of class, but Mr. Harrison didn't pursue things any further, and simply finished with, "Then I suggest you pay attention so that you don't miss anything."

That wouldn't be the case, though, since Jess already knew about food chains. But she waited until his mini lecture was finished and it was time for the students to work in pairs before she filled Miranda in about her knight in shining armor. She eased in at first to test the waters. Searching her memory for any previous conversations she might have had with Miranda that even mentioned Greg in passing, she came up empty-handed, which meant she had no idea what Miranda's opinion of the boy was. For that reason, she went slow, even though her excitement about having a crush on someone Miranda *didn't* have a crush on felt like a tight coil in her chest.

"So I have to tell you something," Jess said, leaning in. She knew this wasn't really secret-worthy on the grand scale of things, but it still felt juicy.

Miranda got excited. "Yeah? What is it?"

"So I walk into advanced English, and Greg—you know Greg, right?"

"Emma's Greg?"

It felt like sprinting *smack* into an invisible wall. Jess attempted to reorient herself. "Um ... I–I don't think so."

"Greg Burns?"

"Yes. That Greg."

"Yeah, Emma's Greg."

Crap. Jess's stomach sank. "So they're boyfriend and girlfriend?"

Miranda nodded. "As of yesterday, yes."

That recently? Of course. *Of course* she would only realize her love for Greg once he wasn't available. And Emma of all people. "I think I'm going to be sick."

"What is it? Did you eat something weird this morning?"

"I guess so." How did she manage to humiliate herself without anyone even knowing what she was humiliated about? Was supernaturally bad timing part of being God's daughter? It seemed so. Even though she'd never read the Bible, she knew enough about it to understand that Jesus never had such poor timing. He'd always been right where he needed to be right when he was needed.

But here she was with the short end of the stick. Maybe all the good timing was used up on her half-brother.

She finally had a serious crush on a boy who wasn't famous and wasn't Chris, and she couldn't even tell her best friend about it. She couldn't decide if she wanted to cry and then throw up or throw up and then cry.

She raised her hand and Mr. Harrison pointed at her. "Yes?"

"Can I go to the bathroom?"

"No, you'll need to wait until after class." He was about to turn back to the board before he paused and looked at her again. "Wait, is it an emergency?" The look he gave her said it all: even Mr. Harrison knew about her period.

A few of the other students snickered when she said yes, but it didn't matter anymore because she was able to leave class. That was all she wanted—to get out and go somewhere away from everyone.

But she also probably needed to change her pad.

She grabbed her backpack and headed out of the classroom, planning to hit the bathroom and then do whatever it took to get out of Marymoore Junior High for as long as possible.

As she entered the bathroom, she shouldered past a couple of seventh graders gabbing by the sinks and parked it inside a stall, hanging her backpack up on the peg and rifling through the front compartment impatiently for a fresh maxi pad. Stupid seventh graders probably had no idea what was in store for them in the next year or so. She could just smite them and their stupid little vaginas.

Hot, angry tears punched their way free from her eyes.

Once she'd disposed of her used pad and replaced it with a new one, *His* booming voice lit up her brain and almost made her tumble off the toilet seat before she could pull up her pants.

THERE IS NO NEED TO CRY.

Oh God!

YES?

No, I mean, get out of here, I'm trying to deal with this.

OH WOW, SORRY.

She pulled up her pants and flushed the toilet, then headed out to wash her hands. The seventh graders had already vacated, which was a small bit of good luck, she supposed.

Okay, I'm good.

WHY ARE YOU CRYING?

Because everything is the worst and nothing matters and everyone hates me.

I KNOW THAT TO BE UNTRUE.

Why did you lie to me?

WHOA, WHOA … I NEVER LIED TO YOU.

You told me I'd have one *friend who would betray me, but turns out it's all but one.*

FIRSTLY, I NEVER SAID **ONLY** ONE. SECONDLY, ALL BETS ARE OFF IN EIGHTH GRADE. EVERYONE KNOWS THAT.

That's not fair.

YOU'RE ABSOLUTELY CORRECT. JUNIOR HIGH IS THE TIME FOR EVERYONE TO LEARN THAT LIFE IS NOT FAIR. IT IS A TIME TO REFLECT ON HOW EASILY PEOPLE CAN DEVOLVE INTO ANIMALS.

You're starting to sound like Jimmy Dean.

THOU SHALT NEVER MAKE THAT COMPARISON AGAIN.

Sheesh. Okay. Sorry. Why is all of this happening?

I THOUGHT THAT HAD BEEN EXPLAINED.

No, I mean with my period. Why did it cause a storm and kill a bunch of cattle?

Silence.

God?

Nothing.

God!

I'M SORRY. THAT, UH, THAT SOUNDS LIKE A QUESTION FOR YOUR MOTHER.

"You gotta be kidding me." *You're uncomfortable talking about menstruation?*

WELL, IT **IS** UNCLEAN.

Why did you make it unclean?

I DIDN'T. I TOLD YOU. I WAS HANDS-OFF WITH THE LADY STUFF.

Fine. But can't you make it clean?

I— HUH. YEAH. I GUESS I COULD JUST DO THAT, COULDN'T I?

Duh!

OKAY. UH. POOF. IT'S CLEAN.

So does that mean I won't have it anymore?

NO, NO. YOU'LL STILL HAVE IT.

Then what's changed?

PLENTY. FOR ONE, OTHERS MAY NOW TOUCH YOU WHILE YOU'RE BLEEDING WITHOUT IT BEING A SIN.

Wait. That was a thing?

TECHNICALLY ON THE BOOKS, YES.

How did you never think to change that until now?

I FORGOT ABOUT IT, HONESTLY.

Of course you did. You really need to talk to more females.

PERHAPS.

The bathroom door opened and Mrs. Thomas walked in. She paused, smiling, but once her eyes landed on Jessica, the faint lines at the corners of her eyes deepened.

"Everything all right?"

Jess stared at herself in the mirror. "Not really." She felt her mind start to clear and knew that meant God had split to leave her in peace. Small blessings.

Mrs. Thomas crossed the row of sinks to lean against

the one next to Jessica. "Want to talk about it?"

"Not really. I just want it all to go away."

She nodded somberly and set a hand on Jessica's shoulder. "I've been there. I understand." She sighed before an idea lit up her face. "Hey, how about you come to my office and relax for the rest of the day, or at least until you feel like going back to class?"

"That's ... allowed?"

Mrs. Thomas chuckled. "I'm the assistant principal, I can do whatever I want." When she grinned, Jess couldn't help but grin back. That kind of power must be nice. Maybe one day Jess could find a way to just do whatever she wanted.

"Yeah, that sounds good." And she followed her out of the bathroom.

Mrs. Thomas had been awarded a new office space this year, one right next door to Principal Mallard's. It felt more like a den than an office, though, with two soft papasan chairs tucked away in a corner, lit by lamps rather than harsh fluorescent overheads. Unlike every other room at Marymoore, Mrs. Thomas's office wasn't overrun with neon posters shouting inspirational sayings about doing your best and being special. Jess appreciated that. Instead, the walls housed long canvases with painted landscapes of places Jess hoped existed because she would like to visit each of them someday.

The scent of lavender wafting from an infuser on the desk helped calm her nerves, and she curled up into one of the scooped chairs as best she could without risking an embarrassing leak. The only part of the decor Jess wasn't

huge on were the framed pictures of Sandra and Fischer on a filing cabinet in the corner. They seemed to stare right at Jess with expressions that managed to be both jovial and snobbish.

Mrs. Thomas lowered her round body into the chair opposite, and before Jess knew it, her mouth opened and words she hadn't planned on saying came tumbling out.

She told Mrs. Thomas all that had happened throughout the day, surprising even herself by confessing her crush on Greg and how she found out he was with Emma.

And Mrs. Thomas nodded along, lending a sympathetic ear that was a luxury Jess had never experienced from an adult before. She imagined telling her mother the things she was telling Mrs. Thomas and was sure Destinee would get so upset halfway through that Jess would be forced to expend her energy talking her mother down rather than continuing with the gory details.

But getting to tell the whole story without interruptions —not even from God—somehow made all the crises of her life feel much more manageable.

"Would you like to go back to class or stay here for a while?" Mrs. Thomas asked at the end of it.

"Stay here." It wasn't even a choice. Mrs. Thomas might as well have asked if Jessica would rather be dropped into the Outback—a place still on God's to-fix list after He'd created it during one of his breaks from tampering with Amazonian bird genes to create more variety (one of His favorite hobbies) and hadn't been mentally present for most of the continent's detail work—or would she rather stay in the lavender-scented haven of Mrs. Thomas's office?

"Okay, that's no problem at all." She sounded like she meant it, too. She stood from the chair and headed over to her desk. "I just need to make a quick phone call."

Jess nodded and let her eyes travel around the room, moving from one detailed painting to the next, while Mrs. Thomas spoke into the receiver in low tones that Jess didn't bother herself with.

The AP hung up the phone. "She's on her way."

"Wait. Who?" This was the first she'd heard of any plan involving another she. Was her mother coming? She wanted to stay in this office for the rest of the day, not go home and have to explain everything to Destinee before starting on her bloody English essay.

"Sandra."

"What? Why?"

Mrs. Thomas looked at her like the answer was obvious. "Because she owes you an apology."

Oh no, not a formal apology. Those were torture. She'd take the Outback over one of those. "But … she wasn't the only one who told, so she shouldn't have to do that."

"That's very thoughtful of you, Jess, but I'm not doing this as an AP, I'm doing this as her mother. You know Sandra can be kind of a … well, a brat. I'm sure it's my fault, but I still have to *try* to correct it."

"It's definitely not because of you." Jess couldn't imagine a better mother to have.

Mrs. Thomas smiled. "Even if that were the case, she owes you an apology."

She felt her armpits moisten as she waited in the silent office for Sandra to arrive.

Then, finally, there was a small tap on the door, and Sandra peeked her head in. As soon as she saw Jess, she bit her lip and looked down at the floor.

While Jess stayed glued to her chair—due mostly to fear of what downpour might happen between her legs if she stood—Mrs. Thomas crossed the room to stand in front of her daughter, who was almost the same height after a late summer growth spurt. "Do you know why you're in here?"

Sandra nodded.

"Well then?"

Sandra sighed and turned slightly to face Jess. It was strange to look at Slinking Sandra right in front of her and Smirking Sandra peeking out from a picture frame over Slinking Sandra's shoulder. Jess's brain couldn't make much sense of it, other than she didn't like it.

"I'm sorry I told people about you starting your period at my party."

"Um. It's okay." Neither Sandra nor Mrs. Thomas moved. Was there something else she was supposed to say? "I ... forgive you."

Sandra's posture immediately jolted straight, her shoulders rolling back like someone had poured ice water down her spine. Her eyes shot open, too, and she stared at Jess with a mixture of fear and awe. "Whoa."

Jess's eyes flickered from Sandra to Mrs. Thomas then back. She was almost afraid to ask. "What?"

"I could feel that!"

Jessica's jaw tightened. "Feel what?"

"It was like ... sparkles!"

No, no... Please no. No more surprises. Please, God, no more surprises.

She shook her head vaguely. "I don't understand." She had a suspicion, but, no, that was too far-fetched. Right?

"Say it again!" Sandra demanded, like a brat.

"Say what again?"

"That you forgive me!" Sandra bounced on her toes.

This didn't seem like how apologies were supposed to go. It was supposed to be a one-and-done thing with the forgiveness. It was just a formality after all. No one *actually* forgave people like Sandra. "I forgive you?"

Sandra moaned, then shook her hands at the wrists. "Yeah! Say it again!"

"No way." It was too weird. She didn't know what was happening to Sandra's body, but she didn't like being the cause of it.

"Do it!"

"No!"

"Sandra," Mrs. Thomas snapped. "Go back to class. Now."

Sandra's eyes glazed over with fear and she turned heel and scurried out of the office.

Once the door closed, Mrs. Thomas sighed and returned to her desk. "That was very big of you to forgive her, Jess. Would you like me to pull Miranda from class to join you for the rest of the day?"

Jess nodded enthusiastically.

Mrs. Thomas looked down at her watch and worried her lip. "Hm." She looked up at Jess. "How do you feel about pizza rolls?"

"Um. I love them?"

"Because I bet if I ordered some now, they'd be here for us to eat by lunch." She beamed before concern overshadowed the glow. "Or, wait. Did your mother already pack you something for lunch?"

Jess's mind traveled to the ham sandwich, tiny Ziploc of plain potato chips, and sliced apple packed into a brown paper bag currently residing in her backpack on the floor next to the chair.

She shook her head. "No, I was just going to grab something from the cafeteria."

Mrs. Thomas's smile returned. "Excellent. An impromptu pizza party it is, then!" She grabbed the phone from its cradle and called Mr. Harrison to have Miranda sent up front.

She paused before dialing the pizza place, held the receiver to her bosom and said, "Don't worry. Eighth grade is difficult for everyone, not just you. It gets easier as you get older, though. Really it does. The trick is to find what makes you happy and focus all your energy on that."

"Does that help?"

"Are you kidding? It makes all the difference."

If she'd heard those words from anyone else, Jess would have dismissed them immediately. But when they came from Mrs. Thomas, Jess dared to hope.

She tried the thought on for size. *Life can be good.* It felt all right. She said it to herself a few more times as Mrs. Thomas spoke with the pizza place, and each repetition felt more convincing.

Now all she had to do was focus on what made her happy and—

Oh crap. What makes me happy?

Nature shows, obviously, but that wasn't normal teenager stuff. Perhaps the matter required more thought ... once she had some pizza in her.

What she did know, however, was a long list of things that made her unhappy—no scratch that, *miserable*: God, the majority of her classmates, her mother's dogged support, menstruation, getting out of bed each morning...

She made up her mind to avoid those things as much as possible, especially that one omnipotent thing atop the list that had put a target on her back since the day she was born.

Maybe if she found a way to distance herself from Him, life would stop feeling like one disaster after another.

I will find a way to be happy. I have to.

Even just thinking the words caused hope to expand in her chest and buoy her spirit.

The first thirteen years of her life had been confusing and scary and chaotic, no question. But even if she only made it to thirty-three before being publicly murdered, she still had twenty more years that she could do with as she pleased. She wasn't even halfway there.

Things will be different. I can be happy. I can be normal.

And in the cozy space of Mrs. Thomas's office, the scent of lavender like a soft blanket around her, Jessica actually started to believe it.

"Pepperoni okay?" Mrs. Thomas asked.

"Pepperoni is wonderful."

Mrs. Thomas grinned widely and nodded. "That's the spirit."

Chapter Eighteen

Jessica inhaled deeply, repeated her new mantra of *You're just Jess,* and walked into Ms. Cantos's English class. She would pretend that seeing Greg was no big deal for her. That her imagination wasn't treating her to an image of Emma putting her filthy paws (oh, who was she kidding? Her *perfectly manicured hands*) all over him, running fingers through his curly mop of hair.

Greg looked up briefly from his book when she sat next to him. "'Sup."

"'Sup," she replied.

Day one of eighth grade had admittedly not been the best in her school career, but now that she knew she could be someone other than the daughter of God and Destinee McCloud if she so chose, she at least felt more in control of her minute-by-minute fate.

She'd also decided that Greg, self-proclaimed atheist that he was, served as a lifeline that she wouldn't yet give up on. He already knew what she was just now discovering:

she was, by most standards, just an ordinary girl. He reflected that back at her in every interaction they had.

So she would make sure they had as many interactions as possible.

"What you reading?" she asked.

Greg's eyes moved to the edge of the page before he pulled them away, glanced over at her, and, with a finger holding his place, closed the book enough to flash her the cover. "*Waiting for Godot*. Samuel Beckett is pretty much a genius."

"Ah, yeah," she said, as noncommittally as possible, since she didn't have a clue.

"Someday I'll write a play this good," he mused. She nodded along dumbly until he added, "Psh. Yeah right!"

"Haha!"

"Oh. My. Gosh ..." came a voice from behind them. It was the last voice Jess wanted interrupting her laugh fest with Greg. It was the voice of Courtney Wurst. "Am I seeing what I think I'm seeing?"

Greg looked at Jessica as if to say, "Oh great, this bitch," which of course he would never say because he was too nice and respectful toward women. He turned in his seat to face Courtney a row behind them.

He didn't say a thing, just waited patiently for the Wurst girl to get this particular bit of awfulness out of her system.

God, he's cool.

"Yes," Courtney said, wagging her finger at them excitedly. "Oh em gee, yes." She paused, making Jess wait before delivering the blow. "She has a crush on you."

Jessica froze, staring daggers at Courtney, a sharp burning sensation erupting behind her eyes.

Thou shalt not smite! Thou shalt not smite!

"Please," Greg said coolly, "we're just friends. Stop trying to start drama where there is none."

Greg had just called her his friend. Greg called her his friend! "Yeah," Jessica squeaked, the feeling in her extremities returning.

He shook his head and turned toward the front. "I swear, Courtney, you must live a boring life if you have to go around listening into other people's conversations and trying to stir up drama."

When he snuck a sideways glance at Jessica, she inhaled oxygen again and then puffed it out, shaking her head like, "Can you believe that girl? *Me* have a crush on *you*? No way. I don't go for dreamy, confident knights in shining armor. I mean, eww, obviously, right?"

She struggled to pay attention to Ms. Cantos's lecture after that. It was a shame, too. Jessica caught just enough details about the various circles of Dante's *Inferno* to be certain that, under different circumstances, this would be an incredibly interesting lesson.

But as it was, Jessica tuned in and out of the content, her mind too preoccupied with how in her Father's name Greg managed to so deftly deflect awkward moments like that, turning them back around on the person intending to inflict them. It was like a superpower. He was a bucket of cold water to fire-starters like Courtney. Before her flame could spread, he doused it completely.

Not only did she want to be *with* Greg, she wanted to *be* him.

After class, Jessica was halfway to her locker before she realized that Greg was walking alongside her. She'd known he was there, but it hadn't dawned on her that *Greg Burns was walking her to her locker.* Because he was so nonchalant about everything, he probably thought nothing of it. But Jessica wasn't blind, and she'd observed, the way any wildlife aficionado might, that when a male and female of the human species walked to the female's locker together, it was an early indicator of a possible mating pair.

That seemed too optimistic to fit her life, though. More likely, Greg was walking with her because he had started on a tangent about something called *Night of the Iguana* and the more she nodded and feigned understanding, the more enthusiastic he became. He wasn't even looking where he was walking. His eyes gazed blurrily toward the ceiling as he talked of disillusionment, whatever that was.

When Jessica paused at her locker, Greg did, too.

"…You know?" he finished.

She did not.

"Totally," she replied. "I never thought about it like that." She briefly considered contributing to the conversation with one of the myriad facts she knew about iguanas. But when she pulled open her locker, anything smart she might have said died in her throat as an avalanche of feminine products tumbled out and to the floor.

Her lungs became petrified wood, her brain an off-center gyroscope. She knew Greg was looking at her—

everyone in the hallway was—but she couldn't do that thing he did, she couldn't glance at him with a smirk as if to say, "Maxi pads? Please. Amateur hour over here. Stuff my locker full of tampons and *then* get back to me about being embarrassed."

She was embarrassed. Humiliated.

Thou shalt not smite! Thou shalt not smite!

Greg didn't say a word.

Her smooth, articulate hero was speechless.

Someone *else* had something to say, though ...

"You think that'll be enough to last you the afternoon, or should I find more?" Courtney's voice came from right behind her. Admiring her own handiwork, no doubt.

The inside of the locker was leak proof, lined with opened pads covering the walls and door. Jessica ripped one off, stuck it to her palm, and whirled around, stuffing it as hard as she could into the face of Courtney Wurst.

Jessica knew, as soon as she felt a slight crunch against her palm, that she'd put just a little too much *oomph* behind the jab.

Courtney's head snapped back and her hand flew up to clutch her nose a moment before her yelp echoed through the hallway. She paused, stunned, before removing her hand from her face to inspect it.

Oh crap.

A river of blood streamed from Courtney's snub nose, flowing over the crest of her top lip and into her mouth. She smacked her lips in disbelief before aiming a murderous look at Jessica.

Sandra, who stood just behind Courtney, leaned around

to glimpse the state of her friend's face, and when her eyes found the blood—it was hard to miss—she gasped. Perhaps she'd meant for the gasp to be one of horror, but the excitement in it was unmistakable.

Jessica had stepped in it now.

"Here," Jess said, offering the maxi pad. "For the blood?"

It seemed like the courteous next step after her miscalculation, a peace offering even.

But as it turned out, it was both the best and worst response to the situation.

It was the worst because Courtney's watering eyes *whooshed* into two blazing infernos of pure hatred; this would bite Jessica in the butt eventually. No doubt in her mind.

But it was the best because Greg, and many of the other students who had stopped to watch, attracted like mosquitoes to a porch light the moment the feminine hygiene products tumbled from her locker, broke into gales of uncontrollable laughter.

One tiny sixth-grade boy shouted, "Ohhh!" with his hand cupped over his mouth. Two seventh-grade girls started clapping enthusiastically.

And as Courtney sprinted away with her head tilted back, pinching her nose, Greg turned to Jessica, a half-grin glowing on his round face, and said, "Okay. *That* was contrapasso."

It was *what*? Did Greg speak Spanish?

"I didn't—" Deciding not to finish with, "mean to do

that," she doubled down. For love. "I didn't know she'd bleed so easily."

Greg shook his head in reverent disbelief. "Damn, Jess. Who knew you had this side to you?"

The warning bell for the next class rang, and he patted her on her upper arm. "See you later."

As he walked away, the glow of the past few moments flickered then went dark.

She'd smacked Courtney Wurst in the nose. She hadn't meant to, not really. She'd only meant to ... what? Shove a maxi pad in her face? They were thick ones, maybe overnights. That should've cushioned the blow a little, but it hadn't. Clearly.

This was *not* how to make oneself less killable.

As she shuffled slowly toward her next class, a voice over the intercom told her something she already knew: Jessica McCloud was wanted in the assistant principal's office.

She shut her locker, leaving the sanitary debris in a scattered pile on the ground, and trudged to meet her deserved fate.

She thought back to her mother's ass-whooping of Mrs. Wurst. Destinee had avoided punishment only because of Jessica's divine gossip about Ruth's affair with Jimmy.

While she wished God would drop in and give her some other piece of blackmail to avoid what lay ahead, she knew she couldn't have it both ways. She couldn't be ordinary only when it suited her. She had to be it all the time.

And ordinary girls didn't get to punch other ordinary (albeit awful) girls in the face without punishment.

Chapter Nineteen

Jessica heard it the moment her mother crossed the threshold into Marymoore Junior High. It was like the starting gun fired, and the runners were off. Except, Destinee wouldn't approach this with the practiced focus of a sprinter—inhale, step-step, exhale, step-step. Destinee's approach to conflict was more roller derby than track-and-field.

The silence in Mrs. Thomas's office minutes before, where Jessica had been allowed the opportunity to explain her side of the story, was pregnant with disappointment. Jessica had wished for any interruption to stop the guilt from consuming her. But nope, maybe not *any* interruption.

Destinee's voice echoed through the halls of the administrative offices. "Where y'all got her locked up?"

Mrs. Thomas shut her eyes, pinched the bridge of her nose, and exhaled deeply, deflating before she sucked in air to ready herself for Destinee's onslaught. That was wise, Jessica thought. The pharmacy was on the other side of town, meaning Destinee had had a full ten minutes on the drive over to get worked up. That was more than ten times the amount necessary for her to transform from accommodating customer service rep to full-blown spree killer.

The door burst open, bouncing off the bumper on the wall and flying back. Destinee charged into the room so quickly she managed to avoid the rebounding door hitting her as it slammed shut. She stopped just short of Mrs. Thomas's desk, not sparing a single glance for her daughter. "That brat had it coming!"

"Mrs. McCloud, please sit do—"

"Jessica ain't done nothing I wouldn'ta done for her!" That seemed to mark the end of Destinee's prepared statement, and Mrs. Thomas's calmness clearly disarmed her. Had she assumed Mrs. Thomas would yell back? Or had she *hoped* Mrs. Thomas would yell back?

The assistant principal did nothing of the sort. Instead, she cleared her throat and folded her hands in her lap, reclining in her padded rolling chair. "Yes, Mrs. McCloud. That's part of what I wanted to talk with you about this morning."

Destinee's face remained taut with aggression, but she took a seat next to her daughter, opposite Mrs. Thomas, as Jessica cast a lamenting glance at the unoccupied papasan chairs in the cozy lamplit corner of the office.

Mrs. Thomas proceeded once Destinee was settled. "Mrs. McCloud—"

"I ain't never been married and I ain't your elder, Dolores. Don't call me that."

Mrs. Thomas bit her top lip before resetting. "Destinee. I want to be upfront with you. Your daughter *was* bullied today."

And every other day, thought Jessica.

"There was also an instance yesterday," Mrs. Thomas continued, "and I'd believed it was settled and wouldn't happen again, but I was wrong."

"No shit," Destinee said. "You think you can stomp out bullies with a few harsh words? Hell no. They don't respond to nothing but being *made* to shut up." She turned to Jessica. "What'd the little Wurst bitch—"

"Destinee!" Mrs. Thomas scolded. "You do not get to call my students that!"

"And you don't get to let those little bitches bully my daughter. But here we are."

Jessica couldn't breathe. She wanted to melt into the floor.

Destinee turned to her. "What happened, baby? What'd they do now?"

She tried to find the words, but she wasn't sure where in the story to begin, so she sputtered, "I-I— They—"

"A student stuffed Jessica's locker with sanitary napkins so that when she opened it, they fell out."

Destinee's head jerked back, and she scrunched up her nose. "Huh?" Then it sunk in. "Oh, that's fucked up."

"And then Jessica proceeded to punch Courtney Wurst in the nose."

"Good," said Destinee.

"I didn't mean to punch her in the nose!" Jessica

protested. "I just meant to cram one of the pads into her face. I don't know why. I was just so angry."

Destinee seemed confused by the subtleties of the situation. It wasn't a clear-cut ass whooping. It was much more nuanced. "It's all right if you socked her in the nose, baby."

"*No,*" Mrs. Thomas said, her calmness eroding as her shoulders lifted up toward her ears. "That is *not* all right. Fighting is not the solution to our problems."

Destinee stood, her hands balled into fists. "It damn well is when it comes to the Wursts! Those bitches never learn unless you make 'em learn! Like mother like daughter, I say!"

Jessica bristled at that proclamation. While Destinee did raise a good point about the Wursts, she didn't appreciate the implications as they pertained to her own situation.

Mrs. Thomas responded to Destinee's bombastic display with a pensive, "Mmm … I see."

It occurred to Jessica that the idea of "like mother like daughter" might be as personally unappealing to Mrs. Thomas as it was for her, though for the opposite reason.

"We seem to have different opinions on the matter," Mrs. Thomas said. "How you choose to discipline—or *not* discipline—Jessica is up to you. However, as her assistant principal, I deem violence as unacceptable beha—"

"You deem bullying unacceptable, too? If you're gonna suspend Jess, you better fucking suspend that pug-nosed brat who started this."

Mrs. Thomas rolled her shoulders back. "Courtney will

be disciplined for her inappropriate behavior. Rest assured. I find her actions as distasteful as you do."

"Clearly not," Destinee grumbled, folding her arms over her chest as she remained standing.

Mrs. Thomas ignored that. "And Jessica will not necessarily be suspended."

"Not necessarily?" said Jessica and Destinee together.

"No," Mrs. Thomas said. "Contrary to your belief, Mrs. McCloud, I do sympathize with bullied students. Just because I've learned to control my emotions doesn't mean I don't get angry, enraged even. I sympathize with the anger Jessica felt, and because she's young and hasn't had the same time to learn self-control as I have—and as you have —I'm willing to overlook her impulsive reaction. Under one condition."

Destinee lowered slowly into her chair. Perhaps it was the possibility of this ending peaceably that subdued her, but Jessica could spot the exact moment the dial in Destinee's head was turned down from *ass-whooping time* to *let's hear this out and see if it's ass-whooping time.*

"Which is?" she asked.

Mrs. Thomas smiled for the first time since Jessica had entered her office. "I'm glad to see we might reach a satisfying, nonviolent resolution. I believe we can downgrade this transgression to in-school suspension, which does not need to go on her record, so long as it's clear to me that Jessica regrets her actions and recognizes that resorting to physical violence is *not* the right approach to conflict. Even with a Wurst."

Destinee blew a raspberry and waved a hand

dismissively. "Well, that's just a load of overeducated horse shit. She said she didn't mean to do it! She ain't got nothing to apologize for, even by your standards. You seriously telling me that if students keep bullying her because your *harsh words* didn't do jack shit, she's just supposed to stand there like a punching bag? Come on, Jess," she said, rising from her chair again, "let's go home. I'm hangry as hell. We'll stop by Gordon's for a burger."

But Jessica remained seated.

She looked from Mrs. Thomas to her mom then down at her feet. Two large drops of Courtney Wurst's blood stained the white fabric of her left shoe. The words "like mother like daughter" echoed in her head, and a delicious phantom scent of Gordon's waffle-cut fries tickled her nostrils.

Ordinary girls didn't rely on God to bail them out of their mistakes. And girls who didn't want to be judged by their mother's actions didn't repeat those same actions.

Mrs. Thomas offered her another option, though. Would it be better? Probably. But even if it weren't, at least it'd be different. And she was just that desperate.

All she had to do was reach out and take it. All she had to do was show remorse. And, perhaps as extra credit, feel remorse.

"Jessica," prompted Mrs. Thomas gently.

Destinee's arms were crossed again, a leg kicked out to the side as she bounced on her toes impatiently.

Jess returned her eyes to the blood on her toe. Being special had never gotten her a damn thing outside of misery. Jesus was special, and look where it got him:

ultimate misery. He probably ended up in the biblical equivalent of the assistant principal's office a few times himself.

What would Jesus do?

Oh, who gave a crap! No one ever stuffed *his* locker full of pads.

She lifted her head but couldn't meet Mrs. Thomas's eyes as she said, "I shouldn't have punched Courtney. That was wrong. Violence is wrong."

"Oh for fuck's sake..." Destinee said on an exhale. She chuckled dryly. "There you go, Dolores. You got what you wanted. You won."

Jess tried to sneak a glance at her mother, but Destinee only had eyes—murderous eyes—for Mrs. Thomas.

"This wasn't a competition," Mrs. Thomas said gently. "And if there is a winner, it's Jessica."

A deep growl rumbled in Destinee's chest, and she took a quick step forward, causing both Mrs. Thomas and Jessica to lean away from her. But Destinee didn't lash out. Not physically, at least. She knelt by Jessica's chair and spoke to her daughter in a voice that reminded Jessica of a feather comforter spread over a bed of nails. "Baby, I ain't mad at you, okay? I disagree with your decision here, but I ain't mad. Not your fault Dolores is part of the reason why the world sucks and the bullies always win. I gotta go back to work, but I'll bring Gordon's home for dinner."

She stood, spun around, and smacked her palms on the desk. Mrs. Thomas didn't even flinch.

The two women were locked in a wordless battle, and

Jessica accidentally found herself begging her father to not allow Destinee to punch Mrs. Thomas right in the nose.

In a deep, guttural voice, Destinee ended the standoff with, "Don't think I don't know what you're doing here. This whole goddamn town has done its best to destroy me over the years, but it ain't gonna happen. You think you can turn my only daughter against me?" She stood, staring down at Mrs. Thomas. "You can go straight to hell."

Mrs. Thomas rolled her eyes. "Mrs. McCloud, I have no intention of turning—"

The office door slammed shut and Destinee was gone.

And a stifling sense of having crossed a line she couldn't uncross hovered around Jessica like a thick smog.

Mrs. Thomas shuffled papers on her desk. "O-kay. Well." She looked up at Jessica, pushing back a conspiratorial grin. "That wasn't so bad, was it? Unpleasant, yes, but I'd say making the right but tough decision *and* getting a Gordon's burger for dinner isn't a terrible outcome, considering."

The smog thinned, and Jessica giggled nervously. "Yeah, I guess."

Mrs. Thomas's casual demeanor was no small comfort. For a moment, the situation in her office had felt like an omen for the End of Days. Then suddenly, *poof*. Jessica had made it through.

And Mrs. Thomas was right; it wasn't so bad. And now she was just an ordinary, independent person. It was like she'd passed through the deepest circle of hell, with Mrs. Thomas as … Virgil? She thought that was right. (She'd pay more attention in Ms. Cantos's class from now on.)

"Your mother has had a hard life," Mrs. Thomas said, expressing an unexpected bit of sympathy for the woman who had, moments before, appeared on the verge of punching her between the eyes. "She does her best."

"You're not mad at her?"

"No, no. Of course not. I do feel sorry for her, though. That doesn't mean I agree with her, but I understand why she is the way she is. It's important you understand it, too, if you want to avoid repeating her mistakes."

Like mother like daughter no more.

Jessica nodded. "I'll try."

"For what it's worth, Courtney refused to apologize for her part and has been suspended because of it. I know it doesn't help the humiliation, but you're clearly the bigger woman here."

Jessica shrugged. "It kinda helps."

There was a sparkle in Mrs. Thomas's eyes when she leaned forward, elbows on the desk, resting her chin on intertwined fingers, and said, "Okay, Jessica McCloud. So you've decided to step out of your parents' shadows and be your own person. That's all very impressive. But now the question is"—she paused, a playful grin stretching her plump lips—"who are you?"

End of Book 1

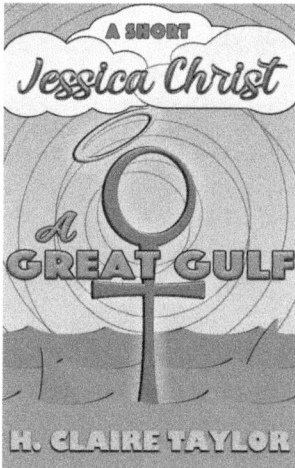

Take a road trip with Jessica, Destinee, and God to visit Grandma McCloud on the Gulf Coast.

Join H. Claire's email group, The Collective, to download this short story for free and treat yourself to an extra dose of humor.

Go to: www.hclairetaylor.com/collective to receive yours

Bonus: And It Was Good

15 AGC

Jess could remember hearing the German language spoken only two times before she found herself in Berlin. The first was in eighth grade world history when Ms. Salinas showed them videos from old Nazi Germany. The second was one night, a year later, when she'd heard her mother crying and shouting at the television while she was trying to finish up homework. Jessica had peeked her head in to see what the matter was only to find her mother sobbing, eyes red and swollen, as she implored Jess to never trust men because they were all evil and corrupt. Since that obviously didn't explain anything, Jess was forced to investigate further, and when she looked at what was playing, she saw more Nazis—better looking ones overall than those in history class—and a little girl in a red coat. Destinee had shooed Jess away after that.

But now she was nestled in a small nook toward the

back of a sunlit cafe, and the German being chattered around her seemed much less threatening and death-related. In fact, it seemed happy, but of course she couldn't be sure, since she didn't actually understand any of it.

Even if she understood it, though, she wouldn't have listened to what those around her were saying, because all her attention was focused squarely on the gorgeous bad boy seated opposite her, his hazel eyes staring intensely back at her from underneath his dirty-blond hair as he spun her a tale of the last time he'd visited Berlin for work and how he'd hardly gotten a moment's respite from the onslaught of his eager fans and how much he appreciated her ability to keep a low profile around him. That was cool of her, he said. Really cool of her.

"I don't know," he continued, as a beam of sunlight caught his eye, "it's just nice to finally talk with someone who understands me."

"For sure," she replied. She braced her chin on her fist as she leaned forward over the small table. He was already leaning forward, and their lips were only half a foot apart as they stared into each other's eyes, a silent conversation taking place that Jess could simply *feel* in her chest.

She'd known the instant he looked at her back at the ... train station?—right, they'd run into each other at the train station—that he was seeing *her*, not God's daughter, but *her*.

It was almost too unbelievable, sitting here having a chat with Jameson. Her friends would never believe it when she told them. She should take a picture of the two of them as evidence. She leaned to the side to check her pockets for her phone, but it wasn't there. Maybe she'd left it back at ... the hotel. Right. She had a hotel. The phone was probably there.

"Hey," he said, his deep husky voice drawing her attention back to him, "have you ever thought about acting?"

"Acting? Not really, why?" Her eyes darted around the cafe for someone who might have a phone and be willing to take a picture. Her need for it was becoming increasingly frantic. If Sandra saw a picture of Jess and Jameson together, it might actually kill the snobby girl.

She needed to find a camera. No excuses.

Jameson seemed oblivious to Jess's search as he crooned on. "I have this new movie coming out, and they're casting for my love interest. I think you'd be great for it. If I put a good word in for you, the part would be yours."

Which person to ask for a phone? And then once she got the picture, would she just email it to herself, or ... ?

She felt Jameson's warm hand on her chin as he gently tilted her face back toward his. "Is that something you'd be interested in?"

Wait, what was he talking about? She rewound the past few seconds in her mind and remembered. "Oh, definitely. I'd love to star with you."

A hunger surfaced in his expression as he narrowed his eyes slightly and inhaled deeply, his nostrils flaring almost imperceptibly. He closed the rest of the distance between them and his lips pressed against hers, briefly but enough to make her forget all about getting a photo. What she was interested in pursuing *now* was something she wanted no one else to see.

He pulled away only an inch. "You want to get out of here?"

"Hell yeah. Let's get out of here."

She glanced up over Jameson's shoulder toward the entrance of the cafe, and that's when she saw the strange man enter. His dark skin and black hair made him stand out against all the blond, light-skinned Germans. Jameson was tan, but this stranger was *tan*. A large nose jutted out above the circle of thick, coarse facial hair on his chin, jaw, and upper lip, and even his clothes were different from the other patrons'. An off-white linen robe covered him from shoulders to ankles, below which small leather sandals peeked out with each step he took toward Jess and Jameson. He seemed to recognize her and made a beeline. And then it clicked.

A terrorist. She was sure of it.

She'd only ever seen men like him on the news when they were blowing up buses and buildings. Or both at the same time.

"What is it?" Jameson asked, turning in his seat to follow her line of sight over his shoulder.

"Watch out, Jameson!"

But the terrorist was cutting across the room too quickly. Jess scooted out of the booth as fast as she could and urged Jameson to do the same so they could escape the nook before anything exploded, but before she could adequately convince Jameson their lives were in danger, the terrorist grabbed her by the back of the arm and spun her around to face him.

"Let me go!" She struggled, trying to free her arm from his grasp. Why was no one helping her? She didn't know how to call for help in German. Maybe they didn't have a word for it. That would explain a lot of the '30s and '40s. She tried to scream, but no sound came out. What the heck?

"Jess," the terrorist said in perfect English.

Her eyes snapped to his face and she gave up trying to struggle, which wasn't working so well anyway. "How do you know my name?"

"You ... don't recognize me?" he asked.

She looked him up and down and shook her head. "Should I?"

"I assumed ... huh."

"Are you not a terrorist?"

"A terr—no! I'm Jesus, you idiot." He let go of her arm and she stumbled back a step.

"Jesus?"

Jameson stood from his seat. "Maybe I should just ..."

"No!" she snapped. "You sit your ass down till we figure this out!" There was no way she was letting him go anywhere until she got either photographic evidence or sex, unexpected Jesus appearance or no expected Jesus appearance.

Jameson sat.

She turned back to her half-brother. "Why are you here?" Then, "*How* are you here?"

Jesus gestured toward a chair at the table next to the booth. "May I?"

She shrugged resignedly. "I guess."

He pulled the chair up to the end of the table, shifted his robes, and straddled it backward, leaning forward, his arms resting on the chair back.

"This is a dream, Jess."

Ugh. Of course it was. Every time she met Jameson Fractal it turned out to be a dream. This had just been the first time anything physical had happened.

And now everything made a little more sense—why she didn't remember what events transpired to get her to this cafe, let alone Berlin, how she and Jameson came to be sitting together, the fact that she couldn't find her phone, and, oh yeah, Jesus Christ.

"Okay, so this is a dream. Perfect." She scooted into the booth next to Jameson before climbing on top of him so she straddled his lap. Since it was a dream, she could engage in any amount of embarrassing behavior and it wouldn't matter; she'd eventually wake up and the slate would be wiped clean. She might as well enjoy herself in the meantime.

She looked down into those sparkling hazel eyes and saw a lusty fire equal to her own staring back at her. She lowered her lips to his, and while her brain didn't quite fill in all the blanks, since she lacked experience in this particular skill, she knew on an intellectual level that she was making out with Jameson, and that would have to do. It didn't even bother her that her half-brother was watching. It was totally worth it to be able to knock this off her dream bucket list.

Please don't wake up yet, please don't wake up yet ...

Jameson wove his fingers through her hair, pressing her lips more firmly to his.

Jesus cleared his throat. "Um. Listen. I'm not here to be a voyeur; I actually have important information for you."

Groaning, Jess pulled her mouth from Jameson's. "But you're not even real. This is *my* dream."

"No, actually, I am real."

Jess plopped herself down onto her butt in the booth. "First of all, that doesn't make any sense. Second of all, if there's something I need to know, God can just tell me."

"Wait," said Jameson. "Aren't Jesus and God basically the same thing? Or two parts to the same whole?"

"No," said Jess and Jesus.

Then Jesus added, "That doesn't even make any sense."

Jameson shut his mouth.

"I don't know if you've noticed this yet," Jesus said, "but our Father who art in Heaven hates the detail work." He paused then quickly added, "And He thought I needed a job, so He promoted me to miracle management."

Jess squinted at him, trying to absorb his words. "Promoted you to miracle ... ?"

"Miracle management," he finished quickly for her. "Yes. When a miracle needs to happen, I show up and tell the person they need to make it happen."

"This is stupid," Jess said, shaking her head.

Jesus shrugged. "What can I say? Nobody likes their job. Doesn't matter. I'm here for a purpose."

"Miracle management," Jess said tiredly.

"Exactly. I'm here to tell you that the time has come for you to stop screwing around."

"That's not very nice."

Jesus held up his palms and nodded his head softly. "I understand. I didn't want to hear it either."

"Wait. Were you told in a dream, too? Who was head of miracle management before you? I don't suppose we have any other siblings I don't know about."

"Not yet. But it was actually Moses who told me. And let me tell you, he didn't put it as nicely as I have. That guy … phew! Meany."

"Meany?" Jess echoed vaguely. "Wait, but if you work his job, what's he doing?"

"Retired."

That made sense in a nonsensical sort of way.

"Anyway, you need to start exploring your special abilities," Jesus said. "There are miracles you can perform, and it's time for you to discover them."

"Miracles? Like how?"

Jesus thought for a moment. "Well, mine were things like turning water into wine, attracting a bunch of fish for a fisherman, bringing people back from the dead …"

Jess nodded along as she began to understand. "Superpowers."

"What? No." Jesus narrowed his eyes at her, annoyed. "Not superpowers. *Miracles*."

"What you described sounds an awful lot like superpowers."

"Well, they're not. Superpowers aren't real. Miracles are."

"Sounds like semantics," said Jameson.

Jess mouthed *I love you* to him, and he returned the favor with a sexy head nod.

"So will one of my superpowers be that I can have sex with Jameson?"

Jesus pinched the bridge of his nose. "Miracles, and no. Having sex with that man is not one."

Typical. Never the good stuff. "So why can't you just tell me what my miracles will be, so I can get on with this dream?"

"Because," he said, increasingly impatient, "there's such thing as self-discovery, and it makes for a much better story."

Jess rolled her eyes. "Ugh. You too? Dad's obsessed with 'telling a good story' and all that. Why does it even matter?"

"Your story is everything! Do you want to be a messiah or not?"

Jess looked at Jameson and chuckled while jabbing her thumb in Jesus's direction. "*This* guy." She turned back toward her half-brother, responding with, "I think I've been pretty clear that I *don't* want to be a messiah. I want to be a normal girl who has sex with Jameson Fractal. That's all I want."

"Well too bad. I–I'm done here. Just figure out your miracles, all right?"

"Whatever." She jumped back onto Jameson and pulled

his mouth to hers. Their lips met and his hand began moving up her torso, toward her breasts that had finally decided to exist, as of the beginning of the dream, and she felt herself grow dizzy with the sexuality radiating off of him. His hand cupped the underside of her breast and she woke up.

Her bedroom was dark, she was alone. No Jameson, no Arab Jesus, just herself and the darkness.

"God. Dammit."

Want to keep reading? The rest of *And It Was Good* is just a few clicks away.

Get yours at:
bit.ly/JCbook2

About the Author

H. CLAIRE TAYLOR has lived in Austin since the eighties (it's her hometown) and hasn't yet found a compelling reason to move away.

After being a Very Good Student™ of creative writing at Texas State University, she worked an assortment of unfulfilling jobs until her inner tortured artist could recover from four soul-crushing years of academia, at which point she held her nose and jumped into the muddy waters of writing comedy full time.

Now she shares a home with her husband and two black-and-white mutts and suffers from an unhealthy dependency on Post-It Notes that she can quit whenever she wants. Really.

When she's not working on her novels, she does professional story consulting, reads about serial killers, and thinks way too much about the paranormal.

Casually stalk her:

www.hclairetaylor.com

Also by H. Claire Taylor

The Jessica Christ Series

The Beginning (Book 1)

A Great Gulf (short story)

And It Was Good (Book 2)

It's a Miracle! (Book 3)

Nu Alpha Omega (Book 4)

It is Risen (Book 5)

In the Details (Book 6)

Kilhaven Police (w/Brock Bloodworth)

Shift Work (Book 1)

Same Old Shift (Book 2)

Wimbledon, Kentucky

A Single's Guide to Texas Roadways

See all at www.hclairetaylor.com

Find more funny books at www.ffs.media

www.ingramcontent.com/pod-product-compliance
Lightning Source LLC
LaVergne TN
LVHW051038080426
835508LV00019B/1589